4-15-94

To my good friend Roger Smith

Hugh Bolton

In the Spirit of Service

Telecommunications from the Founders to the Future

J.D. Frailey and James M. Velayas, Ph.D.

Columbia Creek Publishing
St. Louis

Printed in the United States of America

Frailey, J.D., and Velayas, James M.
    In the Spirit of Service: Telecommunications from the
    Founders to the Future
    J.D. Frailey and James M. Velayas, Ph.D.

    Includes bibliographical references.
    Includes index.
    ISBN 0-9637104-1-9
    Library of Congress Catalog Card Number: 93-72024

This book is dedicated to the millions of men and women who have embodied the spirit of service in telecommunications for over 115 years. Their efforts have brought the human race into closer contact, and helped make the world a better place.

Contents

Part One
The Heritage of Service

Part Two
The Service Ethic Today

Part Three
Service After Divestiture

Foreword

by Glenn E. Watts

Retired President,
Communications Workers of America

The break-up of AT&T was a wrenching experience for virtually all persons employed in the Bell System. It was a shock to industry experts. It has been a mixed blessing to customers, providing lower long-distance rates but at the same time generating new or higher charges in other areas. Service quality meanwhile runs the gamut from top-notch to questionable.

From the vantage point of hindsight it becomes clear that long-standing industry rate structures along with escalating developments in technology would have wrought a dramatic change in the industry—probably in the Bell System itself—even had the Consent Decree divestiture not taken place. Theodore Vail's end-to-end service concept, which resulted in the development of a natural monopoly regulated in the public interest, made use of cross-subsidies to keep residential and rural rates low by charging higher than compensatory rates for business service and for long distance. Even small independent (non-Bell) telephone companies were subsidized out of the national network pool for "division of revenues."

While this was good for persons receiving the subsidies, those paying the higher rates became potential targets for would-be competitors. Large profits could be made so long as the competitor could "cream skim" and was not obligated to serve and subsidize rural and residential service; with technology making transmission cheaper and easier, all that was needed were changes in the laws that protected the local telephone companies' monopolies.

The first crack in the dam was the 1968 CarterPhone case, in which the U.S. Supreme Court required access by other parties be permitted through the telephone company networks. Large customers threatened to "do their own thing" unless they received lower rates than those available through the regulated companies. Some threats were carried out, others were not, but they were omens of the future. The development of the "Teleport" concept in Florida, New York, and other locations added to the mounting evidence that a big thing was sure to happen to the Bell System. The MCI antitrust case found against AT&T certainly played a large role in the ultimate AT&T management decision to accept the now famous Consent Decree.

It has now been nearly a decade since the clock struck midnight on the Bell System, and one of the greatest organizations ever to serve humanity passed from existence. Careers have been altered or terminated, lives and families have been turned upside down, and thousands of jobs have been lost as the industry shake-up has proceeded. The U.S. economy lost billions of dollars when the internal non-tariff barrier of self-contained manufacturing and supply within the Bell System was dropped without hearing or legislative action; the U.S. market, the largest in the world, was flooded with instruments from abroad, and today no telephones are made in the United States.

And still the evolution of technology continues unabated. Its effects are awesome. Consider the impact of telecommunications technology on the world. As it did in the Bell System, it can be credited with contributing to the "divestiture" of the former Soviet Union, and with the growing turn to democracy and market economies in the former Eastern Block countries. Technology is irresistible and inevitable; its effects can be managed, well or poorly, but they cannot be stopped.

In their book, In the Spirit of Service: Telecommunications from the Founders to the Future, J.D. Frailey and James M. Velayas take the reader from "Mr. Watson, come here, I want you!" to the life and death struggles of the early days of the industry, to a tribute to the unique spirit of service that lives on in the Telephone Pioneers of America. The authors conclude with an eye-opening year-by-year review of the people and events shaping the new AT&T and the Regional companies, from the 1984 divestiture to the present. The overriding theme throughout the book is that the service ethic made this industry great, and the degree of adherence to the spirit of service will—more than anything else—determine its fortunes in the uncertain future.

Glenn E. Watts

Authors' note: Mr. Watts began his telephone career in 1941 as a telephone installer with the Chesapeake and Potomac Telephone Company in Washington, D.C. He became active in the Communications Workers of America and worked his way up the leadership ranks, becoming president of national CWA in 1974. During his eleven years at the helm, Union representation climbed from 498,000 to 675,000, and great advancements were made in wages, benefits and working conditions. While a national officer Mr. Watts helped CWA develop collective bargaining relationships in the telecommunications industry to include pattern and national bargaining, especially within the Bell System before divestiture. During the last ten years CWA has moved into programs involving worker participation and a cooperative approach as a preferred solution to today's workplace problems. Mr. Watts retired in 1985 and now lives in Chevy Chase, Maryland. He is active in numerous charitable and community service activities including the Holocaust Memorial Council and the Holocaust Memorial Museum Campaign. He is an honorary member of the Alexander Graham Bell Chapter of the Telephone Pioneers of America.

Preface

This book was originally envisioned as a collection of interviews with industry leaders from the era of divestiture to commemorate the ten year anniversary of that historic event. It was to assemble their recollections of the leadership issues and logistical challenges created by that time of upheaval as well as their assessments as to how the industry has evolved since then.

As preparation we began reading books on the history and heritage of the telephone and of the telephone business. We had spent a combined total of nearly thirty years in telecommunications, yet were amazed to find how little we had previously known about the industry that brought the world the information age. With this new perspective we began to rethink our approach to the book.

That rethinking took shape as we learned more about the heritage of service in the industry and about the Telephone Pioneers of America, the world's largest industry-related community service group. We learned what the Pioneers stand for, what makes them tick, what they symbolize by extension for the entire telephone business. In a word it is *service* that fuels their rockets. Unselfish, dedicated service to others.

We then realized service was the thread that would weave the material in these pages into a cohesive book. Service is what this industry is all about! Anyone who has ever worked in the business, whether the Bell System or other, knows what this means. Anyone who has ever used the telephone in a country other than the U.S. or Canada (and, increasingly, Mexico) can better appreciate the level of service we take for granted until faced with an outage or emergency.

With our sights on a new target we rolled up our sleeves and went back to work. The writing of *In the Spirit of Service* has been both challenging and deeply satisfying. Our hope is that current and retired employees and their families will feel a sense of pride for the contribution this industry has made and continues to make. Other persons with an interest in history or heritage will also find a fascinating story, as will the millions of you who own what are still the bluest of the blue chip stocks. Finally, we trust this book will contribute in some small measure to preserving the memories of those brave and visionary founders whose legacy we honor and whose heritage we share.

J.D. Frailey, St. Louis
James M. Velayas, Ph.D., San Antonio
June 1993

Part One

The Heritage
of Service

The Heritage of Service

Lives of great men all remind us
We can make our lives sublime
And, departing, leave behind us
Footprints on the sands of time.

Longfellow

When we seek to identify factors that create strength, purpose, and a sense of identity among groups of people, we often begin with a look at their past. In order to truly understand someone, ourselves included, we must know something of our heritage. We draw strength and inspiration from the stories of those who went before us. We become connected to something larger than the here and now, and are therefore better able to see our lives and our contributions in perspective. Plus, by honoring and preserving our heritage we keep it alive for those who will follow us.

The fascinating story of telecommunications, from Alexander Graham Bell through the present, will without question be regarded by history as the dawn of the Information Age. This section of *In the Spirit of Service* presents the inspiring heritage of the former Bell System and its current offspring primarily through the stories of five of the founders. To retain as much authenticity as possible, certain selections were taken from rare and classic writings, many of them previously out of print for years.

And now please join us on a journey of heritage and service, starting with the invention of the telephone as told by Tom Watson, Alexander Graham Bell's assistant and the world's first telephone technician.

Thomas A. Watson, 1874

1

Tom Watson, the First Technician

Thomas A. Watson was Alexander Graham Bell's laboratory assistant. His name has become famous because it was included in the first sentence ever spoken over the telephone.

What sort of person was Tom Watson? How did it come to pass that this particular man became a part of history, part of the great heritage of the telephone business? What was it like to work with Alexander Graham Bell on the experiments that resulted in the greatest invention in history, the breakthrough that changed the world more than anything before or since?

A Perspective

Literature on Watson, including his 1926 autobiography, reveals him to have been an exceptional person: bright, enthusiastic, and hard-working. He maintained this perspective his entire life, even after losing nearly his entire fortune from his part in the invention of the telephone. Here, now, are selected highlights from *Exploring Life*, the autobiography of Tom Watson, the Bell System's first technician.

Background and Childhood

After I had attained some notoriety from my role in the invention of the telephone, a genealogist looked up my ancestors. Tracing them back three or four generations, he found farmers, mechanics, laborers, one or two school teachers and a preacher or two. Then he lost the thread in the defective records of New Hampshire towns and could go no further. The most interesting individual he discovered was an ancestor who started the Free Will Baptist Church in the United States. He was probably a strict sectarian, but he handed none of it down to me.

I was born in the center of the good old city of Salem, Massachusetts, on January 18, 1854. My birthplace and boyhood home was a two story and a half, pitch roofed, clapboard, unpainted house. It was in a corner of a stable yard, among the outbuildings, near where the buggies and carriages were washed and painted. Harnesses, carriage robes, and equipment were kept in the lower rooms, and family quarters for eight of us were on the other two floors.

My father was broad-shouldered, muscular, and usually good-natured. He attended to emergency calls for teams of horses coming at all hours. He was on duty from early morning until late at night, seven days a week. We children saw little of him except at mealtime. My mother seldom left home, was quiet, hard-working, and efficient. She and my half sisters kept the house exquisitely neat and clean. They washed, ironed, scrubbed, mended, and cooked all day and every day, winding up the week's work by scrubbing us youngsters in a washtub every Saturday night. There were no conveniences to lighten their labor. All our fuel and water had to be lugged up two flights of stairs from the dark, wet, cobwebby cellar—a duty to which I was introduced at a very early age.

That atmosphere of household drudgery and the constant care I had to exercise not to add to my mother's burdens influenced me all my life in such ways as the meticulous use of a doormat, distress if I tear or soil my clothes or spot a tablecloth. It has also caused me to take great pleasure in any device that simplifies and saves labor. Waste of any kind, whether of labor or material, was always abhorrent to me.

There are also touches of beauty in my recollection of my early home, especially the morning-glories my mother grew in our tiny back yard. Never have I seen any flowers so exquisite as those purple morning-glories trained on strings by the back door, their loveliness enhanced by their otherwise shabby environment.

My only playground was the stable yard and its buildings. I sailed shingle boats in the water trough while the horses snorted at them. From an accessible branch of a great ash tree growing in the stable yard I often watched the activities in the yard below, romancing about the strangers who came there. We played hide and seek in the carriage sheds, but my best fun was in the great hayloft filled with fresh hay in which I and other boys dug long tunnels and played Indian.

Although a child's environment is undoubtedly an important factor in the development of his character, much with which I came in contact during my impressionable years repelled rather than allured. Brought up in intimate contact with horses and stablemen, the more I saw of the business the less I liked it. I never wanted to drive a horse when a boy and never did like doing so. My father and all the stablemen smoked, but tobacco never was a temptation to me. Nearly every man I knew drank several glasses of whisky and water every day without any attempt to conceal it. Whisky was easily accessible to me but I never cared to experiment with it and was practically a teetotaler all my life.

Education and First Jobs

When I was five years old I was taken to Miss Fogg's private school where very young children were taught for twenty-five cents a week, but I do not remember learning much there. Two or three years later I was taken to a public school and although I have not the faintest recollection of studying anything there, I presently found I could read. After I had mastered that art, reading became one of my principal pleasures.

When I was eleven years old I went to work in a crockeryware store that backed on the stable yard. I swept the store before breakfast and did errands between school sessions and on Wednesday and Saturday afternoons, all for fifty cents a week, which I diligently saved. I held other jobs while in school such as sweeping up in a paper-box factory and as a sales clerk in a ready-made clothing store. At age fourteen, after one year in high school, I quit my early formal education to go to work as a clerk in the crockery store where I had formerly been an errand boy.

After a year or so I began to take night courses in a Boston commercial college, and later became a bookkeeper. I soon lost interest in bookkeeping, however, and decided to learn a trade. I first tried carpentry but found the work too exhausting. I resumed my search and, after a few odd jobs, began just the kind of work I liked at the machine shop of Charles Williams, 109 Court Street, Boston, on July 1, 1872. I was happy there because I had found a trade that would soon enable me to earn three or four dollars a day, which seemed quite all I should need to live on and to save for my old age. Getting this job at Williams's electrical shop was a turning point in my life but I had no premonitions of important events ahead.

Watson Meets Bell

In the 1870's this was a very different world as far as the practical use of electricity was concerned. The principal use of electricity then was for telegraphing and for fire alarms. This required the use of a variety of apparatus—keys, relays, sounders, registers, switchboards, galvanometers, and a few printing telegraph instruments, all of which Williams made and sold in small quantities.

My work was intensely interesting except when several hundred pieces all alike were given me to make. I found such repetition work tiresome at first but soon found a way to lessen the monotony by observing my movements at the lathe or vise, then trying to reduce the motions to the fewest possible. I also blended them so that a new movement began before the previous movement ended, and was careful to use the same sequence of motions for each piece in turn. Such jobs then became nearly automatic and the pieces were finished so quickly that the job lost its tediousness. Elimination of useless movements is now an important part of scientific workshop operation, but I never heard of its being done until years after I had made it a part of my daily routine in the early 1870's.

Before two years had passed I was no longer rated an apprentice but as a skilled journeyman who could turn out work so rapidly that, when slow times came, I was never laid off. More importantly still, although I did not foresee it, my study of work movements and labor-saving devices was to be a large factor in my success as an electro-technician and in my being chosen to do the pioneer work on one of the world's greatest inventions.

After about two years my reputation as a rapid and accurate workman began to bear its most important fruit by bringing me into contact with men who had new electrical ideas they wanted to have made into physical form. The modern development of electrical machinery was just then beginning and many men were studying its possibilities. Williams's shop was a paradise for these men of vision. There were often two or three of them there, feverishly supervising the construction of their machines, spurred on by visions of boundless wealth.

One day early in 1874 when I was hard at work on an apparatus for exploding submarine mines by electricity there came rushing out of the office door and through the shop to my workbench a tall, slender, quick-motioned young man with a pale face, black side-whiskers and drooping mustache, big nose and high, sloping forehead crowned with bushy jet-black hair. It was Alexander Graham Bell, a young professor at Boston University, whom I then saw for the first time.

He was bringing me two little instruments I had made without knowing what they were or to whom they belonged. They had not been made in accordance with his directions and he had impatiently broken down the customary rules of the shop by coming directly to me to have them altered.

To help me understand what I was trying to accomplish Bell explained them to me at once. They were, he said, a transmitter and a receiver of his "harmonic telegraph," an invention of his which he expected would, when perfected, enable him to send six or eight telegraph messages over a single wire simul-

Alexander Graham Bell, 1876

taneously so that one wire could do the work of six or more.

I made for Bell one receiver and one transmitter both tuned to the same pitch. They worked so well when we tried them on a circuit in the attic of Williams's shop that Bell ordered six pairs of the instruments. But when they were finished and we tried to send several messages at once the receivers would not always pick out the right messages. Ultimately we accomplished little of practical value in spite of our hard work over the next several months. The chief result was to prove to Bell that the harmonic telegraph was not as simple as it seemed.

Bell Shares His Great Idea

I had not worked with Bell long before I found the harmonic telegraph was not his only new idea. His head seemed to be a teeming beehive out of which he would often let loose one of his favorite bees for my inspection. A dozen young and energetic workmen would have been needed to mechanize all his buzzing ideas. There was one of Bell's ideas that was easily queen of the hive. I have never forgotten the first time it stung me.

Bell, being busy during the day, would often ask me to stay in Boston with him in the evening to help him test his apparatus. One evening when I had been working with him, trying some new feature in the discouraging harmonic telegraph, he said to me, perhaps to cheer me up a little, "Watson, I've another idea I haven't told you about that I think will surprise you."

I listened somewhat inattentively while I worked away at my instruments. My receptive powers were hardly at their best, for those evenings I stayed in Boston meant an eighteen hour day for me. He then went on to say in his usual convincing way that he had kept an idea in his head for more than a year by which he was sure he would soon be able to *talk by telegraph!* His startling assertion banished my tired feeling and I don't remember that it ever came back.

Bell had a remarkable power for clear and terse explanation. The words he used in giving me the essence of his great idea have remained in my mind ever since. "Watson," he said, "if I can get a mechanism which will make a current of electricity vary in its intensity, as the air varies in density when a sound is passing through it, I can telegraph any sound, even the sound of speech."

The world has not been the same since, nor will it ever be again.

The Big Breakthrough

It was June 2, 1875, a day that stays in my mind as one of vivid contrasts—a black and white, gloom and sunshine, lean and fat, poverty and riches, sort of a day. Bell and I had spent the day in Williams's attic, trying to make the harmonic

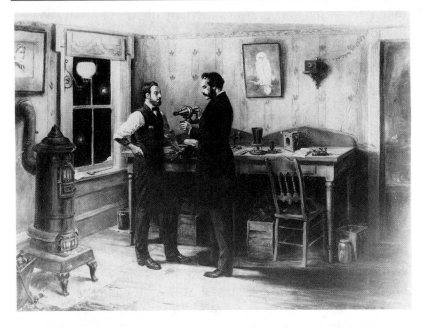

Bell's Exeter Place laboratory

telegraph behave itself. He had found that one reason why its messages got mixed up in transmission was inaccuracy in tuning the receiver reeds to match those of the transmitters. This was always his part of the job for he was a fine musician with an excellent ear, while my sense of pitch was altogether inadequate for such work.

When tuning a receiver reed Bell had the fortunate habit of pressing it against his ear. This enabled him to hear in the magnet the whine of the intermittent current coming from the distant transmitter. By changing the length of the receiver reed with a simple instrument I had designed while holding it to his ear he could harmonize the two pitches.

On that hot June day we were in the attic hard at work experimenting with renewed enthusiasm over some improved piece of the apparatus. About the middle of the afternoon we were re-tuning the receiver reeds, Bell in one room pressing the reeds against his ear one by one as I sent him the intermittent current of the transmitters from the other room. One of my transmitter reeds stopped vibrating. I plucked it with my fingers to start it going; the contact point was evidently screwed too hard against the reed and I began to readjust the screw while continuing to pluck the reed. Suddenly I was startled by a loud shout from Bell and out he rushed in great excitement to see what I was doing.

What had happened was obvious: the too-closely adjusted contact screw had prevented the battery current from being interrupted as the reed vibrated; for that reason, the noisy whine of the intermittent current was not sent over the wire into the next room. Rather, that little strip of magnetized steel I was plucking was generating by its vibration over the electromagnet that splendid conception of Bell's—*a sound shaped electric current!*

Probably nothing would have come from the circumstance if any other man than Bell had been listening at that moment. Bell, with his mind prepared by his great conception instantly recognized the supreme importance of that faint sound. It told him his long-studied idea had at last found its mechanism. He knew he was hearing, for the first time in human history, the tones and overtones of a sound transmitted by electricity, and realized it was being done by some part of his telegraph apparatus. His shout and eager rush into my room was his reaction to that startling realization of his dream.

I want to stress that while the derangement of the transmitter was accidental the invention of the telephone was not an accident! It was an instance of the prepared mind solving a long studied problem by means of an unexpected result suddenly presented during work on a different line. In that way Bell's harmonic telegraph was a success not as a telegraph, but as the means that led to a far greater thing.

The First Telephone

We spent the rest of the afternoon and evening repeating the discovery with all the steel reeds and tuning forks we could find. Before we parted late that night Bell sketched for me the first electric speaking telephone, urging me to do my best to have it ready to try the next evening. As I studied the sketch on my way to Salem on the midnight train I felt sure I could do so.

The first telephone was a very simple mechanism consisting of a wooden frame on which was mounted one of Bell's harmonic receivers. The receiver consisted of a tightly stretched parchment drumhead with the free end of the receiver reed fastened to its center, and a mouthpiece to direct the voice against the other side of the drumhead. It was designed to force the reed to follow the vibrations of the voice and so generate voice-shaped electric undulations.

I made every part of that famous first telephone with my own hands, but I must confess my prophetic powers, if I had any, were not in operation that day. Not for a moment did I realize what a tremendously important piece of work I was doing. No vision of the giant that new-born babe was to be in a few years came to me as I hurried to get it ready to talk. I am sorry I was too busy at lathe and bench to do any dreaming; it would make a good story if I could say now that I foresaw the great things to come and was stimulated by them to work even harder. But there was nothing of the kind; I rushed the work only because I was mightily interested in the invention and wanted to hear it talk.

When Bell arrived that evening, after the men were gone from Williams's shop and we had the place to ourselves, he inspected the telephone and pronounced it quite right. I had strung a wire from the attic to the basement to put greater distance between us so we would be sure anything we might hear was actually coming over through the telephone and not merely through the air. The results were extremely disappointing. Bell, in the basement, could not hear a thing when I shouted into the transmitter in the attic. When we changed places, however, I could unmistakably hear the tones of his voice and almost catch a word now and then.

We tried every way we could think of to make the telephone talk better that night but soon the parchment of its drumhead became softened by our breath. We spent the rest of the night discussing possible improvements in its design and construction, thereby beginning the research work on the telephone that has gone on unceasingly ever since.

It was not until March 10 of the following year that the telephone had been sufficiently developed to transmit a whole sentence intelligibly. This was part of the now famous incident in which Bell, on spilling some diluted acid on his jacket, shouted into the telephone, "Mr. Watson, come here, I want you!" I, stationed at another instrument in a different part of the boarding house where we conducted our experiments, heard every word distinctly.

(Note: The circumstances surrounding the famous night of March 10, 1876, as well as the exact first words transmitted over the telephone, remain in dispute. Bell recorded the first words in his journal as, "Mr. Watson, come here. I want to see you." Further, Bell makes no mention of acid being spilled. Perhaps either Watson embellished the story for the sake of drama, or the very proper Bell omitted the acid incident because he may have regarded it as undignified).

Watson Joins the Team

I signed a contract to work for Bell late in the summer of 1876, for $3.00 per day plus ten percent interest in all of Bell's patents. Several years later, when our financial situation was beginning to look brighter, Gardiner Hubbard said to me, "Well, Mr. Watson, that contract you made with us was a good thing for you." After a pause and with a twinkle in his eye he added, "And a good thing for us, too."

And he was right both ways. I received about 60 telephone-related patents in my name; as per my contract with Bell and his associates they became the property of my employers, although I received ten percent of any proceeds. As it turned out, one of my patents on telephone apparatus was worth to the Company all I got from my contract; it was a favorable arrangement for everyone including me.

The Power of Perseverance

There were, of course, many disappointments, as is nearly always the case in the pursuit of anything of great significance or value. I would estimate our failures outnumbered our successes by at least a thousand to one. But there is infinite power in right thought coupled with perseverance, I believe, that eventually overcomes even the most obstinate and pervasive of difficulties.

We had our disappointments but were rarely discouraged. There were enough promising glimpses of success that we knew we were on the right track. It was a matter of trial and error, adjustment, refinement, then more trial and error. When things became discouraging Bell had a way of booming out, "Watson, we are on the verge of a great discovery!" and my tiredness would vanish and the work would continue.

When you know you are on the right track never give up. Never quit! The power of perseverance has been proven so many times it is above question. Anyone who has ever achieved anything of lasting value, almost without exception, did so in spite of repeated failures; it was and is the power of perseverance that wins the day.

Western Union Blows It

As is often the case in life, the biggest letdown turned out to be the biggest blessing, and it involved the value of the enterprise. With the beginnings of formal telephone lines in 1877 the financial burden was getting more and more troublesome. Thomas Sanders of Haverhill and Gardiner Hubbard of Cambridge, the two men who were paying for literally everything associated with the venture, were impatient for some returns. They had offered to the Western Union Telegraph Company all of Bell's telephone and harmonic telegraph patents for one hundred thousand dollars.

Western Union evidently had no faith in the future of the telephone for they refused to buy the patents and wouldn't even make an offer for them. I was quite excited while these negotiations were going on and much disappointed when president Orton of the telegraph company finally and somewhat contemptuously turned down our offer.

There was reason for my excitement for I would have received about ten thousand dollars as my share. I also expected a position with the telegraph company as superintendent of their telephone business. But their rejection of Hubbard's offer turned out to be another piece of good fortune for us all. Two years later those same patents could not have been bought for twenty-five million dollars!

Reflections on Alexander Graham Bell

History gives us many illustrations of the transforming power of an idea, but Bell's conception of a speech-shaped electric current ranks among the most notable of them. The conception itself was the great thing; if Bell had never found the apparatus for which he was searching to produce his ideal current, his name should still have been immortalized.

No finer influence than Alexander Graham Bell ever came into my life. He was the first educated man I had ever known well and many of his ways delighted me. His attentive courtesy to everyone was a revelation. The books he carried in his bag lifted my reading to a higher plane. He introduced me to authors and scientists of whose writings I had been ignorant. He scolded me for dropping my algebra and bought me the latest book on the subject he could find.

The best thing Bell did for me—spiritually—was to emphasize my love for the music of the speaking voice. He was himself a master of expressive speech. The tones of his voice seemed to vividly color his words. His clear, crisp articulation delighted me and made other men's speech seem uncouth. When he learned of my interest in speech tones he was surprised and pleased and gave me some of his father's books on elocution. He pointed out errors in my way of using my voice, all of which I keenly appreciated. I diligently practiced what he had taught me when I went into the woods on my Sunday walks.

Another thing I found most interesting was Bell's table manners. Up to that time, the knife had been the principal implement for eating in my family and among my acquaintances. The only point of table etiquette that had ever been impressed on me was that the knife should be put into the mouth with its sharp edge towards the middle as otherwise there would be danger of widening the orifice painfully.

And Bell had another fascination for me: he was a pianist, the first I had ever known. To play the piano had always seemed to me the peak of human accomplishment. It seemed so occult and inexplicable that I asked Bell one evening, when he was playing on his boarding-house piano, if it was necessary to hit the keys exactly in order to play a piece or would striking them anywhere in certain vicinities of the keyboard answer the purpose? My respect for the art was greatly deepened when he said the precise key had to be struck every time.

The Early Telephone Team

Someone has said that the men who controlled telephone affairs in their infancy—Bell, Hubbard, Sanders, and Watson, were just the men for the job, each doing his part of the work without interfering with the others, together making a smooth running machine. It would not be modest of me to fully endorse this judgment, but as far as the rest of them are concerned I can do so heartily. Gardiner Greene Hubbard's function was of the highest importance. His keen, visionary mind conceived many of the fundamental policies which are still an essential part of the telephone business.

Thomas Sanders was our treasurer, and we could not have had a better one. Had it not been for his never-failing pluck and optimism, Bell and the rest of us might have missed the prosperity that came later. I think he would have hardly rated as a conservative businessman, and it was lucky for us that he was not; had he been, he would never have risked his fortune as he did to supply us with funds in those uncertain years.

Thomas Sanders

I knew other young electricians who could have done
my work with Bell as well as I did it, but there was only one
Bell with his big idea. My principal value as his associate was,
perhaps, that I hastened the development of his idea into a
commercial success. Possibly by so doing, I averted the danger, rather imminent at times, of his losing much of his financial reward. Bell was a pure scientist; making money out of his
idea never seemed to concern him particularly. But there were
many ingenious minds hungry for profits, ready to seize for
their own benefit any hints Bell might let drop. Had there been
a delay of a year or two in the commercializing of Bell's conception the history of the telephone business would probably
have been very different from what it is.

The Business Grows . . . and Grows

In April of 1877 there had been only six telephones in practical use, with that number growing to three thousand by November. At the end of that year we found we were to have a competitor; the growing number of telephones in use had finally convinced Western Union that Bell's invention was a good deal more than a toy. Since the Bell patents were no longer for sale Western Union started into the business anyway, ignoring our patents. This was a tremendous source of pressure and stress to us all.

In February 1878 I made my first trip West to inspect the telephones that were in use, to convince our agents to establish central offices, and to find out what the Western Union people were up to. My route took in Chicago, Milwaukee, Pittsburgh, Washington, and all the larger cities along the way. I found our telephones giving fairly good service although I found neither telephones nor bells had been cleaned or adjusted since they left the shop; my time on this trip was largely spent showing our agents how to keep the instruments in order and arranging for their regular inspection. The trip gave me a new realization of the colossal nature of the telephone business and of the work still to be done to put it comfortably on its feet and able to hold its own against competition.

On May 21, 1878, I started on another, longer tour of inspection and instruction. On this trip I first met Theodore Vail. Mr. Hubbard had felt for some time that there was too much of a load on me and had been looking for someone who would relieve me of all except the engineering work. He was enthusiastic over possibly hiring Mr. Vail but before deciding wanted me to meet him. For this reason my first stopping place on this trip was Washington, where Mr. Vail had his office as superintendent of the United States Railway Mail service.

Mr. Vail and I had a long talk about the telephone business and I think what I told him was a factor in his decision to come with us. I was sure he was the right man for us and was delighted at the prospect of getting rid of the parts of my work

34

I didn't like. I telegraphed Mr. Hubbard to hire Mr. Vail if he could see his way to paying him the large salary he wanted, thirty-five hundred dollars a year! Before I returned from this trip Mr. Vail had been engaged as our general manager.

Alexander Graham Bell to the Rescue

In 1878, as soon as it became evident the telephone was likely to be a financial success, bitter litigation began over Bell's patents. By fall of that year all parties to this suit except Bell had filed their statements and it was necessary for him to do the same at once. But he was still in England, where he had gone on his honeymoon with his bride Mabel. He was also demonstrating the telephone and attempting to garner interest in its use abroad. Letters from him indicated he was having a hard time there, and that he was disgusted with the telephone business and determined to have nothing more to do with it.

In October he wrote that he was leaving England, was going directly to his father's house in Brantford, Ontario (where Bell had conceived the original idea for the telephone) and wasn't coming to Boston at all. Our lawyers warned us that Bell must come to Boston immediately to preserve his rights. We knew from his letters that he was utterly indifferent to the whole matter, and we realized that unless we acted quickly he would be too late to save the situation.

On November 8, 1878, I went to Quebec and waited until the 10th, when the steamer arrived with Professor and Mrs. Bell, his baby girl and nursemaid. I found Bell even more dissatisfied with the telephone business than his letters had indicated. He told me he wasn't going to have anything more to do with it, but was going to take up teaching again as soon as he could get a position. I gave him as clear a picture as I could of what we had accomplished in the United States, painting the future of the telephone business there in bright colors.

I must have made some impression on him for he finally said he would go to Boston with me after he had taken his wife and child to his father's house in Ontario. I went with him for I didn't want to run the risk of losing him. We stayed there

35

several days before I succeeded in getting him started for Boston. He would not go until he had received an answer to a telegram he dictated and had me send to Boston, which read: "Will Company pay Bell's expenses incurred in its service to Boston and back?" Of course the answer was "Yes."

Bell was sick and had to go to bed as soon as he got on the sleeper. On arrival in Boston he went to the Massachusetts General Hospital for an operation. His preliminary statement, dated November 20, 1878, was made while he was there but it was filed in time and, perhaps, saved his patent.

Bell hadn't been with us many days before he realized the telephone business in the United States was vastly more promising than it was in England and likely to be such a financial success that it would not be necessary for him to teach for a living. He recovered from his sickness in a few weeks, but aside from his testimony in this suit and others that followed he took no further active part in the telephone business. He had other inventions in mind to which he preferred to devote his time.

After the Telephone

I resigned my position with the Telephone Company in the spring of 1881 at age twenty-seven. The same desire for a larger life and new experiences that had improved my fortunes by sending me from the crockery store into the machine shop was stronger than ever. Further, my interest in the telephone had diminished rapidly as the lonely, fascinating, pioneer work I had been doing, covering the entire field of telephony, had necessarily been more and more divided among many workers.

I imagine that if I had obtained in my youth what was then considered higher education my appetite for study would have been satisfied and I would have been contented to stick to one job all my life. But my early schooling, limited and poor in quality, had done for me the best thing any school can possibly do: it turned me out with an insatiable desire to know more.

If I had stayed in the telephone business my life would

Watson in 1881

have been easier and my income larger, but I would have missed many experiences which, although some of them were hard to bear, built into me something of everlasting value.

After 1881 neither Bell nor I played a noteworthy part in the great development of the telephone into the instrument of universal service it has become. This has been done by those who followed us, by the new pioneers—by the work of thousands of trained men and women coordinated with consummate skill into an organization almost incomprehensible in its complexity, size, and scope, with its thousands of central offices, its tens of millions of miles of wire which connect millions of telephones in every nook and corner of the world. Those wires pulsate day and night with speech carried by those sound-shaped electric waves conceived by Alexander Graham Bell.

37

Postscript

Watson's life had many ups and downs after he left the telephone business. For the first two years he traveled throughout Europe, seeing the sights, learning the languages, and soaking up the culture. When he returned to the U.S. he bought and operated a farm near East Braintree, Massachusetts. He spent much of his time there inventing labor-saving farm machines and tools in a workshop in his barn.

It was in that workshop that he became interested in steam engines and eventually started the Fore River Engine Company, which later became the Fore River Ship and Engine Company. Over a period of twenty-two years Watson guided Fore River to become the largest shipbuilding company in Massachusetts. Huge amounts of capital were required to keep such an operation afloat, however, and Watson eventually depleted all his telephone stock and other savings for that purpose. When government defense contracts dried up after World War I Watson found himself on the wrong end of a forced sale; he was bankrupt except for a small trust he had established years earlier.

His business and money were gone but Watson's focus remained not on his losses but on the future. At the same time he was proud of the role his ships had played in helping the Allies prevail in World War I, and of the 20,000 jobs which had contributed $130,000,000 to the Massachusetts economy in Fore River's nearly quarter century of operation.

Watson bounced back from losing his business and savings by staying busy, which is a wise path when a person is once again required to earn a living. With his expert knowledge of geology (acquired through studies at M.I.T.) he conducted expeditions, then wrote and lectured on his findings.

He was also helped on the path back by starting each day with 30 minutes of inspirational reading, especially that of Whitman and Emerson, and of Browning, who wrote:

But what if I fail of my purpose here?
It is but to keep the nerves at strain,
To dry one's eyes and laugh at a fall,
And baffled, get up and begin again
So the chase takes up one's life, that's all.

In his mid-fifties Watson followed his dream and traveled to England to fulfill a lifelong ambition: he became an

Watson in "Much Ado About Nothing." Stratford, 1911

actor in Frank Benson's traveling Shakespearean Company, starting at the bottom with apprentice actors half his age. For a year he lived in dingy theatrical boarding rooms, ate generally bad food, and worked long hours doing everything from endless rehearsal to helping build and assemble props.

In spite of the hardships and sacrifices of this new life Watson loved every minute of it. He began to write plays in the little spare time he had. At the end of the Shakespearean tour, when new material was in demand, the director of the troupe was so taken with Watson's writing (as he had been with his spunk and his willingness to do whatever was asked of him) that he and his acting company used Watson's plays for the remainder of their tour. Watson cherished the farewell he received from Benson: "Don't ever lose your eternal youth, Mr. Watson!"

Watson returned to the United States and began a serious study of painting in addition to maintaining his geological expeditions and lectures. He also received countless requests to appear at ceremonial telephone events, including participation in the first transcontinental telephone call, with Alexander Graham Bell, in 1915.

Passage

Watson died in 1934 at his home in Florida, having rebuilt his fortune to half a million dollars. It was small in comparison to what he could have possessed had he played it safe, but he never regretted his choices. He had followed his heart and enjoyed a rich, full eighty years of exploring life.

Portait of Alexander Graham Bell

2

Alexander Graham Bell, a Lifetime of Service

I. Birth, Boyhood and Beginnings

Of all the people who have walked the face of this planet it has been the destiny of only a handful to materially alter the course of human events. The inventor of the telephone (and of much more, as you will see) was born March 3, 1847, in Edinburgh, Scotland. He was christened with the same name as both his father and grandfather: Alexander Bell. The newest Alexander—or Aleck, as he was known—would not announce the addition of his self-chosen middle name, Graham, until his eleventh birthday.

His father and grandfather handed down more than just their names to the boy. Their pioneering work in the study of human speech and the correction of speech defects was instrumental in his interest in the science and transmission of sound. His mother, Eliza Grace Symonds, was a painter as well as wife and mother. She was also an excellent pianist in spite of her deafness. Young Bell acquired his love of music from her, as well as the beginnings of his interest in the education and advancement of the deaf.

Introduction to Science and Inventing

He dabbled at collecting leaves, rocks, and insects, but this soon became boring to him. Later, his interests switched to the more interesting mechanical gadgets of the mid-nineteenth century, especially telegraphs.

His first invention came as the result of mill owner Ben

Herdman, the father of a boyhood friend, advising his son and young Bell to find something useful to do rather than idling their time away at Mr. Herdman's mill. As a result they created a rotating paddle device fitted with brushes to separate grains of wheat from their husks. The contraption actually worked, and was temporarily put into use at the mill. Mr. Herdman gave the boys the use of a workroom where they spent long hours inventing and experimenting to their hearts' content.

The Boy Becomes a Man

In 1862, at the age of fifteen, Bell was sent to London to live with his grandfather as a companion and apprentice. This was the beginning of a year the inventor would describe, a half-century later, as "the turning point of my life." His grandfather tutored him in the customs, manners, and refined speech of

Alexander Graham Bell at 16

European culture, which he adopted easily.

The boy acquired both a strong sense of companionship with his grandfather and independence as a person. When his father came to London to fetch him home to Scotland some months later he found a dignified, studious, and thoughtful young gentleman. In 1863, at the age of sixteen (although he easily passed for several years older), Bell obtained the position of pupil-teacher of music and elocution at the Weston House School for Young Gentlemen in Elgin.

Visible Speech

In 1863 Bell's father achieved his greatest accomplishment, the development of a universal phonetic alphabet he called Visible Speech. Many others had been searching for such a breakthrough, but after fifteen years' effort Alexander Melville Bell got there first.

Rather than using the standard alphabet characters A-Z, Bell's system employed symbols for each sound a person might make. These symbols represented various positions of the tongue and lips, the shape of the mouth, and the correct use of breath. Visible Speech made it possible to communicate any sound a human being is capable of creating.

Alexander and his brother Ted became experts in the use of their father's system and served as his assistants in public demonstrations. It would later be through Visible Speech that Alexander Graham Bell would achieve his remarkable successes in teaching the deaf to speak even if the person had been deaf from birth.

Coming to America (via Canada)

In 1870, after both his brothers had died from tuberculosis, Bell's grieving parents decided to move to Brantford, Ontario. Their only remaining child, now twenty-three years old, reluctantly agreed to go with them.

In April 1871 Bell moved to Boston, a city he and his father had visited two years earlier to promote Visible Speech.

Boston School for the Deaf, 1871.
Bell is at the top of the steps on the right.

He obtained a position at the Boston School for Deaf Mutes and resumed the teaching he loved so much.

His method of teaching the deaf to speak began with a simple exercise: he drew a human face on the chalkboard and had the children point to their own ears, eyes, mouth, and so forth, as he pointed to the corresponding features of the face on the board. He then erased parts of the face until only those features represented in Visible Speech symbols remained, and from there began his teaching. The results he achieved with the delighted children, even the toddlers, astounded the faculty and parents.

From the Dreaming Place to the Big Breakthrough

Life was good for young Alexander Graham Bell. He

alternated between continuing the experiments in the transmission of sound he had begun in Scotland, and teaching the deaf to speak. It was during one of his private lessons that he met Mabel Hubbard, the pretty young deaf girl who would later become his wife. Mabel was also the daughter of Gardiner Hubbard, the man who would play such a critical role in the patenting and commercializing of the telephone.

Bell lived part of the year in Boston and part of each year with his parents in Brantford, Ontario. It was at Brantford in the summer of 1874 that he conceived the fundamental idea of the telephone, at the "dreaming place" on the bluffs above the Grand River near his parents' home. It would be two years later, in Boston, with the help of young Tom Watson, that he would make the telephone talk.

II. Service after the Telephone

What did Alexander Graham Bell do after he invented the telephone? Many people assume he simply rode off into the pages of history on riches and reputation.

Hardly. Having invented the telephone before the age of 30, the remainder of his life was spent providing useful service to his fellow human beings. Bell once said, "Wherever you may find the inventor, you may give him wealth or you may take from him all that he has, and he will go on inventing. He can no more help inventing than he can help thinking or breathing."

Another motivation that kept him going was avoidance of what his Pulitzer Prize winning biographer Robert V. Bruce called, "the deadening handicap of early fame." "I can't bear to hear," Bell once wrote Mabel, "that even my friends should think that I stumbled upon an invention and that there is no more good in me."

"There is no truer test of ownership than the fact of creation," he said. "That which a man makes himself, he feels he owns." In 1876 he wrote Mabel that, "the real reward of labour such as mine is SUCCESS...a medal far more valuable than gold...a medal that you may wear around your heart—and that

The Bells with daughters Elsie and Marian ("Daisy"), 1885

will wear as long as history itself."

Bell's accomplishments after the telephone amount to a tremendous contribution even when considered by themselves. Since claims to the telephone are securely his, however, the rest may be considered icing on a very large cake. What follows here is but a sample.

The Photophone

In 1879 Bell began experiments on what today must be seen as the forerunner of fiber optics, or talking by light. Six years earlier, in England, the discovery had been made that the

Illustration of the Photophone, 1880

electrical resistance of the element named "selenium" is altered by light. "If you insert selenium in the telephone battery and throw light upon it," Bell explained, "you change its resistance and vary the strength of the current you have sent to the telephone, so that you can hear a shadow." Bell intended to transmit speech over light beams, and thereby gain advantage over Edison's then superior carbon telephone transmitter.

He hired a young assistant in October 1879 named Charles Sumner Tainter, who had, like young Tom Watson, worked in Williams's electrical shop, on terms similar to Watson three years earlier: fifteen dollars a week and a one-tenth interest in any of Bell's ideas; Tainter would also retain fifty percent interest in any ideas of his own.

Early success came quickly. Bell's notes record that "the problem of the reproduction of speech was . . . solved by Mr. Sumner Tainter and myself in my laboratory No. 1325 L. St. Wash. D.C. on Thursday, February 19, 1880." One week later he wrote: "I have heard articulate speech produced by sunlight! I have heard a ray of the sun laugh and cough and sing! . . . I have been able to hear a shadow, and I have even perceived by ear the passage of a cloud over the face of the sun's disk. . .Can Imagination picture what the future of this invention is to be?"

Having learned the importance of documentation and secrecy prior to patent applications being filed, in early March Bell and Tainter sealed a model of the Photophone in a tin box, along with a detailed description of their work on the device to that time. They then delivered the box to the Smithsonian Institution for safekeeping. Bell's excitement was obvious. He wrote a scientist friend that his secret invention would "prove far more interesting to the scientific world than the telephone, phonograph, or microphone." He sent money to an English cousin for him to discretely purchase small amounts of selenium at a number of scattered locations so he would have a supply on hand when his invention was made public.

On March 26 Bell and Tainter achieved results over approximately 90 yards. In his journal Bell declared that date as "a Red Letter day for Photophony!" On April 1 they shattered all their records when Tainter transmitted a message 230 yards, from a schoolhouse rooftop to a window of their laboratory. This resulted in the deposit of another box with the Smithsonian containing among other things the historic words transmitted over the new Photophone distance record: "Mr. Bell, if you hear what I say, come to the window and wave your hat." Years later Bell said of that moment: "It is unnecessary to say that I waved with vigor, and with an enthusiasm which comes to a man not often in a lifetime." He added that such moments are, "worth a lifetime to live for."

In a paper for the American Association for the Advancement of Science, Bell unselfishly credited the Photophone's development as being largely due " . . . to the genius and perseverance of Mr. Sumner Tainter." He went so far as to give himself second-billing in the subtitle: "Researches of Sumner Tainter and Alexander Graham Bell."

The National Bell Telephone Company did buy the rights to the Photophone for a modest sum, although fondness for the inventor of the telephone likely had as much to do with the transaction as did perceived practicality. "Whether this discovery ever approaches the telephone itself in practical importance or not," president Forbes of National Bell said, "it is no less remarkable and a thing which we should be glad to possess."

As it was, the Photophone never saw widespread application; its range remained limited, and even then was generally dependent on sunny days. In 1897 Marconi jumped far ahead in the wireless game when he transmitted radio signals over a distance of several miles. Yet, in 1921, less than a year before his death, Bell told an interviewer: "In the importance of the principles involved, I regard [the Photophone] as the greatest invention I have ever made, greater than the telephone."

Influence on the U.S. Census

Throughout his life, when asked his occupation, Bell (whose wife and mother were both deaf), always responded, "Teacher of the deaf." He also made significant contributions in support of the deaf in many areas besides teaching.

In 1878 Bell was contacted by the Massachusetts Board of Health, which persuaded him to help in its effort to gather statistics on deafness in order to better understand the laws of heredity. Bell soon discovered that, while interest in the study of human heredity was on the rise, available data was lacking. Beginning in 1879 Bell provided financial support to a long-term study to gather statistics on tendencies toward deafness in the offspring of both deaf and hearing parents.

Bell himself remained active in the research arena, and by so doing made a valuable contribution to the preservation of history by helping shape U.S. Census policy. In 1886 he discovered the forms from the first U.S. census, conducted in 1790, littering the floor of a vault under the U.S. Patent Office; more than 1,000 volumes were already in such bad shape as to be worthless. He lobbied the Secretary of the Interior, who promptly agreed to have them rescued and properly stored.

In 1889 Bell reported he found the census documents "invaluable" for genealogical research, although they had apparently never been used for this purpose. Today, the use of census documentation is standard practice, but it was Alexander Graham Bell who showed the way.

The Practical Phonograph

In 1880 Bell received the French government's Volta Prize for scientific achievement in electricity for his invention of the telephone. The prize, established by the first Napoleon and named for the Italian scientist Alessandro Volta, was considered by Bell as the greatest of all the honors he was to receive. With the 50,000 francs that accompanied the award (equal to $10,000 U.S. at the time) Bell established the Volta Laboratory in Washington. He persuaded his cousin Chinchester Bell, who was an expert chemist, to move to the United States from England to join Tainter and him in the effort.

Their project of favor was to apply a healthy dose of one-upsmanship to Thomas Edison, whose carbon telephone transmitter had earlier wreaked havoc on Bell's telephone interests. But now Edison had neglected his own invention, the phonograph, to concentrate on electric lighting. The phonograph remained a laboratory plaything, its flimsy foil recording surface becoming ruined after only a few playings. What was needed was a means to transform the phonograph into something durable that would lend itself to mass production. In the spring of 1881 the Volta Laboratory came up with the idea of applying a permanent magnetic field which would reproduce sound through a traversing pickup. This became, essentially, the seed that would grow into modern tape recording.

Two goals were set by the group: quality sound reproduction and increased durability. The Volta associates decided to try grooves cut into some easily carved material, selecting wax for this purpose. Edison himself had at one time listed wax among the possibilities for a recording material, but his documentation was sketchy. Later, the courts ultimately held for Sumner Tainter's explicitly worded patent, which became the most valuable single output of the Volta Laboratory.

Other improvements to the phonograph were made by Volta, including the floating stylus, such that it is fair to say they made the phonograph practical and thereby brought music to the masses. Bell's profit from the phonograph was placed in a trust to be used for research relating to the deaf. This seed money is still at work today in the form of the Alexander Graham Bell Institute for the Deaf in Washington, D.C., and through that organization's publication, the *Volta Review*.

The Telephonic Probe

Bell's attention was temporarily diverted from the phonograph on July 2, 1881, when U.S. President James A. Garfield was shot in the back by Charles J. Guiteau. The bullet did not kill Garfield, but rather, as biographer Bruce put it, "that work was left to the doctors, a procession of whom began almost at once to insert unwashed fingers into the wound . . ." Bell and the Volta associates directed their energies into work on a device to help locate the bullet, starting with the "induction balance" invented by David Hughes, a friend of Bell.

On July 23, after the president's condition had worsened, Bell and Tainter brought their apparatus into the White House through a private entrance in order to avoid the reporters who had learned of the experiment. The procedure failed, but Bell was deeply moved by the scene in Garfield's

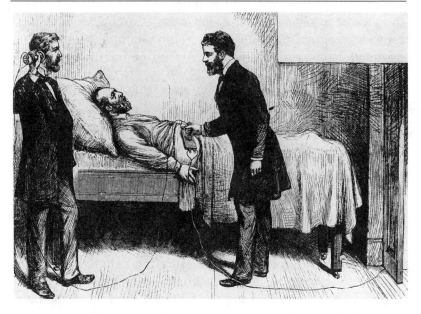

*Illustration of Bell attempting to locate a bullet
in President Garfield*

sickroom and re-doubled his efforts to help.

Work at Volta Laboratory continued nearly around the clock, with Bell, Chester, and Tainter pushing themselves to the brink of exhaustion. Then Bell shifted direction and created a "needle probe," consisting of a telephone receiver and two electrodes. One electrode was a metal plate held against the patient's skin while the other was a thin needle, all but the tip coated with shellac, for insertion into the patient's flesh. A click would be heard through the telephone receiver if the needle touched the bullet.

But by then Garfield was very weak, his weight having fallen from 200 to 120 pounds, and the doctors decided not to try the new apparatus. On the night of September 19, in Washington, Bell learned of the death of the president from a newsboy outside his window. The autopsy revealed the bullet was too deep to have been detected by Bell's probe, anyway, and that its position was actually harmless. Garfield had died from infection and from a ruptured aneurysm caused by either the entry of the bullet or by the surgeons poking around in the wound.

There is, however, a happier twist to this otherwise tragic story. In October 1881 Bell successfully demonstrated the telephonic probe to a group of physicians. Dr. John Girdner attended the demonstration, and later began using and publicizing the device. As interest in the probe spread, Girdner wrote Bell saying, "I have never nor could I lay any claim to the originality of these inventions." But Girdner's next paper on the subject did not even mention Bell's name. The early nineties saw advertisements for "Dr. Girdner's Telephonic Bullet Probe," and his 1933 obituary declared him" the inventor of the Girdner telephonic bullet probe, which was used universally for the removal of bullets before the development of the X-ray."

Bell showed no sign of being perturbed by Girdner's attempt to steal the spotlight, probably since Girdner's publicizing the probe had increased its usage and therefore undoubtedly saved many lives. The telephonic probe saw service in the Sino-Japanese War of 1894-1895, the Boer War of 1899-1902, and even to some extent in World War I. The medical establishment made sure history acknowledged Bell as the rightful inventor, however. In 1886 the University of Heidelberg awarded Bell an honorary M.D. degree for his contribution to surgery, and in 1915 Bell was given full credit for the telephonic probe in the British Medical Journal.

The National Geographic Society

Founded by Bell's father-in-law Gardiner Hubbard in 1888, the National Geographic Society remained a small, ho-hum, primarily scientific organization during Hubbard's lifetime. Its dry, somber journal, the *National Geographic Magazine*, attracted a small circulation.

When Hubbard died in 1897 Bell was, in his words, "forced to become the president of the National Geographic Society in order to save it." But experiments and other interests absorbed him during his first year of "saving it," while membership dropped from fifteen hundred to one thousand and debts began to pile up. At that point Bell got busy. The solution, in his opinion, was to transform the dreary dull publication into a bright, non-technical magazine that would appeal to a more general readership, and to hire an energetic, intelligent, full-time editor. Bell offered to underwrite the editor's $100.00 monthly salary.

When the Board accepted the offer, Bell, accompanied by his daughter Elsie, persuaded young Gilbert Grosvenor (the "s" is silent) to quit his New Jersey teaching job to become the first full time employee of the National Geographic Society. The Bells had come to know Gilbert as the son of Professor Edwin A. Grosvenor, a guest lecturer brought before the Society in 1897 by Hubbard. Professor Grosvenor had taught history at Constantinople for twenty years and was the author of a copiously illustrated book on that city. Whether Elsie Bell's accompanying her father on a recruitment trip to persuade young Gilbert to take the editor's post had anything to do with his decision is not clear; it should be noted, however, that they were later married and had a long and happy life together.

In a series of letters during the summer of 1899 Bell offered young Grosvenor advice on building the magazine's circulation to "thousands instead of hundreds." The magazine should have "a multitude of good illustrations and maps," he wrote in July.

Bell urged the young editor to take advantage of the free materials available through the many scientific bureaus in the Washington area. He urged the use of maps, of making the magazine "of so much value to the schools that it would be used as a sort of text book of current geography."

Bell also urged the new editor to emphasize a truly national and expanded membership by, among other things, including a blank form for the nomination of new members in every magazine, a move which proved highly successful.

At the end of the first year of Grosvenor's editorship, circulation had doubled to twenty-four hundred, and he received a raise of $800 per year. The young editor resisted outside advice to increase circulation further by switching from an emphasis on membership in the Society to newsstand sales. In 1904, when membership leaped from 3,400 in January to 11,000 in December, Bell ended his subsidy. "There is no reason why the membership should not reach ten times ten thousand," Bell wrote his then son-in-law, "in which case the magazine would become one of the most important and influential journals in existence." The hundred thousand mark would be reached in only eight more years.

Years later, in reminiscing on his career, Gilbert Grosvenor credited his father's book on Constantinople, with its 200 illustrations, as the chief inspiration for the magazine's phenomenally successful format. But after Bell's death in 1922 Grosvenor wrote that he had kept Bell's letters of advice and instruction written in 1899 and 1900 before him "as a chart in all the ensuing years." When Gilbert Grosvenor retired as editor he was succeeded by his son (and Bell's grandson) Melville Bell Grosvenor, who was later succeeded by *his* son, also named Gilbert ("Bert") Grosvenor. Bert Grosvenor has relinquished the editorship but remains president of the National Geographic Society.

Mankind's Gift of Wings

Bell had been fascinated with flight ever since his youth, watching the soaring seagulls from the cliffs of his native Scotland. Mabel probably rekindled that interest when she wrote him from Washington in April 1891: "I wish you were here if only to attend the National Academy meetings and to hear the discussion on Professor Langley's flying machines." Samuel P. Langley was a self-educated physicist, director of the Allegheny Observatory, professor of physics and astronomy at the Western University of Pennsylvania, and secretary of the Smithsonian Institution. He and Bell became close friends and Bell permanently caught the flying fever when he witnessed a demonstration of Langley's model airplanes in June of that year. "They FLEW for me today!" he wrote. "I shall have to make some experiments upon my own account in Cape Breton. Can't keep out of it!"

If small machines could fly, as he and so many others (including the Wright brothers) reasoned, why not a full-sized machine capable of transporting people? But many leading scientists of the day thought the concept of manned flight impossible and even preposterous. These doubters included the celebrated British scientist Lord Kelvin, who expressed to Bell "regret that he was going into aeronautics." Undaunted, Bell plunged into what would rank as among the most challenging and consuming work of his life.

He experimented with flight for years, much of this with giant kites constructed of numerous tetrahedral triangle cells covered with red silk; in flight, they made for a beautiful and dramatic scene against the sky above the kite field at Beinn Bhreagh (pronounced "Ben VREE ah," Gaelic for "Beautiful Mountain"). Beinn Bhreagh was Bell's home for 37 years and is located just outside the village of Baddeck, Cape

The main house at Beinn Bhreagh, Baddeck,
Cape Breton Island, Nova Scotia

Breton Island, Nova Scotia. "I have traveled around the globe," Bell declared. "I have seen the Canadian and American Rockies, the Andes, the Alps and the Highlands of Scotland, but for simple beauty Cape Breton outrivals them all."

Although his success with kites was limited, Bell's innovative kite designs cleared the way for expanded use of the strong, lightweight, easily mass-produced tetrahedral cells. Tetrahedrals would later be adopted world-wide for construction projects ranging from bridges to buildings.

On October 1, 1907, Bell and his wife Mabel formed the Aerial Experiment Association (AEA) at Baddeck, for the purpose of attaining manned flight within one year. Included in the group, which was to operate for one year with $20,000 capital supplied by Mrs. Bell, were four bright, energetic young men: Casey Baldwin, Glen Curtiss, Thomas Selfridge, and J.A. McCurdy. These four also served as surrogate sons for the Bells, whose only two biological sons had died as infants in 1881 and 1883. The small group grew very close during their time at Beinn Bhreagh, working hard during the day, then sharing stories and song with the night owl Bell.

They were also not without their setbacks and heart-

Flight of the Silver Dart, February 1909

breaks. In September 1908 Thomas Selfridge became the first fatality in aviation history when a two person airplane in which he was riding crashed in a test conducted for the military at Fort Myer, Virginia. The pilot, Orville Wright, was badly injured but survived. Mabel offered to put up another $10,000 for a six month extension of the AEA, as its one year duration was about to end. The others accepted, feeling it only appropriate to keep up their efforts in light of Selfridge having made the ultimate sacrifice in the pioneering of aviation.

The six month extension would prove to be enough. The AEA ultimately achieved its stated goal in grand fashion on February 23, 1909, with the half mile flight of the Silver Dart. The flight was piloted by McCurdy at the speed of forty miles an hour over the frozen lake at Beinn Bhreagh. The flight of the Silver Dart has gone down in history as the first manned flight in Canada, and the first by a British subject on British soil. Alexander Graham Bell, Selfridge, and Curtiss have all been inducted into the Aviation Hall of Fame in Dayton, Ohio.

The Vacuum Jacket

As a result of the tragic death of his infant son, Edward, from respiratory failure in the summer of 1881, Bell invented a device for helping people breathe through artificial respiration. It consisted of an airtight cylinder fitted around the person's torso up to the neck, with air forced in and out by means of a suction pump. When air was pumped out of the chamber the person's lungs were forced to expand and air entered through the mouth.

Bell saw the device as a means of reviving victims rescued from drowning, but this did not pan out due to the emergency nature of such incidents. What Bell did not foresee was the use of his vacuum jacket combined with an external power source for persons requiring indefinite treatment. This use would find its greatest need years later with the outbreak of polio, when Bell's vacuum jacket would evolve into the lifesaving iron lung.

Hydrodomes

In 1906, as a result of his work with aeronautics, Bell became interested in the idea of adapting and applying the "lift" principles of airplane wings to boats, which had earlier been tested with boats under tow. Water resistance is a major hindrance to boat speed; if small "wings" under the water could lift the boat up as it traveled, Bell reasoned, water resistance would be decreased and speed would increase. Bell decided to call this new breed of boat the "hydrodome."

Bell watches the HD-4, 1919

Hydrodome experiments began at the lake at Beinn Bhreagh in 1908. The first craft, the HD-1, was completed in 1911. After redesign and renaming as the HD-2, it reached a speed of 50 miles per hour in 1912.

In 1914, following the pre-World War I rumblings in Europe, Bell stepped up work on these craft. He believed a perfected hydrodome would prove valuable in military service;

while opposing war, he was also committed to shortening it by helping the Allies win.

Experiments continued, with advancements coming in small steps but coming nonetheless. Bell's perseverance kept things moving through years of setbacks and disappointments. The culmination of his work was the HD-4, a long, cylindrical craft with tapered ends resembling a huge cigar. On September 9, 1919, at Beinn Bhreagh, the HD-4 set a marine speed record of 70.86 miles per hour, a mark that would stand for a decade.

In retrospect Bell seems to have been ahead of his time with hydrodomes. They did not see action in World War I after the military instead decided to use a combination of aircraft and small boats to do the work Bell had envisioned for them. But in the 1950's these craft, now called hydrofoils, began to gain in popularity. Numerous hydrofoils may now be found in service around the globe.

These are but a few of the contributions by the man you may have previously thought of as merely the inventor of the telephone.

Hardly.

Thank you, Mr. Bell.

Passage

Alexander Graham Bell died on August 2, 1922, at his beloved Beinn Bhreagh. He died of diabetes in the very year insulin was discovered, only months before this life-giving extraction became available and may well have brought the longevity Bell had always predicted for himself. His wife, Mabel, passed away six months later.

During his funeral, on August 4, all telephone service in the United States was intentionally stopped for one minute. Flags were flown at half mast on all Bell System buildings, and the entire world mourned the passing of this great man. Thomas Edison, who had from time to time been a rival of Bell, now spoke in tribute of "my late friend, Alexander Graham Bell, whose world-famed invention annihilated time and space, and brought the human family in closer touch."

Bell and Mabel, Beinn Bhreagh

III. A Hand for Helen Keller

The story of Alexander Graham Bell and Helen Keller is reprinted with permission from Bell: Alexander Graham Bell and the Conquest of Solitude, by Robert V. Bruce.

Among the deaf were those people who, like Mabel Bell, insisted they would rather live sightless but warmed by voices in the dark than encased in the cold, bright solitude of deafness. Among them also were those for whom even the solitude was dark. They were the deaf-blind.

Bell knew the deaf-blind, too. In February 1876 he had attended a memorial service to the late Samuel Gridley Howe, the educator and reformer who had done pioneer work with the blind. Howe had been head of the Perkins Institution for the Blind in Boston, and his most famous pupil there had been a deaf-blind student named Laura Bridgman. At the age of two Laura had lost her sight, hearing, even most of her sense of smell and taste. Little remained to make her living body more than the sealed tomb of her mind. But Howe had touched that mind and found it responsive. And so Laura had discovered the existence of the world and had learned something of what it held. At the service for Howe, Bell had "quite a little talk" with Laura—by means of finger spelling—and as Bell wrote at the time, Laura had cried for her dead teacher. "The whole scene was one I shall long remember," Bell wrote.

Years later, in 1887, Captain Arthur H. Keller, a former Confederate officer who had become a newspaper editor in Tuscumbia, Alabama, brought his six-year-old deaf-blind daughter Helen to Bell in Washington. Helen was a healthy child, excited to something like happiness by what she sensed of the novel journey. Bell may have seen irony in the contrast between her eager gropings and her father's sadness. Yet in her well-shaped face, for all its intimations of dormant intelligence, there seemed to be an indefinable, chilling emptiness. Bell listened to the story of the illness that had left Helen completely deaf and sightless at nineteen months. Something in his touch, Helen remembered years later, gave her an impression of tenderness and sympathy. She sat on his knee and felt his watch strike. He understood her rudimentary signs, and she knew it and loved him at once. "But I did not dream," she wrote in later years, "that that interview would be the door through which I would pass from darkness into light."

According to Helen, Bell unlocked that door with the suggestion that Keller write Michael Anagnos, at that time the director of the Perkins Institution. As it happened, Anagnos was already prepared. A friend of Keller's had spoken to Anagnos about Helen's case months earlier, perhaps at the insistence of Helen's mother, who had read about Laura Bridgman in Charles Dickens' *American Notes*. Then, on the strength of a tentative inquiry from Keller himself in the summer of 1886, Anagnos had alerted one of his star graduates to the possibility of such a call. She had since been studying Howe's carefully recorded methods in the case of Laura Bridgman and spending much time with Laura. Presumably Bell's encouragement in February 1887 rekindled Keller's interest or settled his doubts about Helen's educability. At any rate Keller wrote again to Anagnos and thereby initiated the astonishing lifework of Annie M. Sullivan.

Annie was then twenty years old, still haunted by the horrors of her four childhood years in the Tewksbury poorhouse, still suffering from the effects of trachoma, which had once made and would again make her blind. Still, she was soon to be called by Mark Twain and others the miracle-worker and by Helen Keller simply "Teacher." It was on March 3, 1887, that Annie Sullivan arrived in Tuscumbia. That day was to be cherished by Helen Keller as her "soul's birthday." It also happened to be the fortieth birthday of Alexander Graham Bell.

"A miracle has happened," wrote Annie on March 20; "the wild little creature of two weeks ago has been transformed into a gentle child." On April 5 came Helen's famous breakthrough to the understanding that things had names, and three months later she was writing letters. Bell followed the Tuscubmia "miracle" with wonder, as did the public after Michael Anagnos sounded the trumpet. Bell himself helped to spread the news, furnishing a New York paper in 1888 with

Helen's picture and one of her letters to him. He saw a wider good coming from the dazzling emergence of her mind. "The public have already become interested in Helen Keller," he wrote in 1891, "and through her, may perhaps be led to take an interest in the more general subject of the Education of the Deaf."

In one respect Bell stood alone among Helen Keller's admirers and celebrators. He insisted that what Annie Sullivan and Helen Keller between them had done was not a miracle but a brilliantly successful experiment. "It is . . . a question of instruction we have to consider," he wrote, "and not a case of supernatural acquirement." He interviewed Helen himself to measure her progress and pressed Annie Sullivan for explanations of it, especially of Helen's command of idiomatic English. From what Annie reported, he found the key in the fact that she constantly spelled natural, idiomatic English into Helen's hand without stopping to explain unfamiliar words and constructions and that she encouraged Helen to read book after book in Braille or raised type with a similar reliance on context to explain new vocabulary. This, as Bell pointed out, was the equivalent of the way a hearing child learned English. And it supported his long-standing emphasis on the use of the English language, rather than sign language, with deaf children. Indeed, he saw the importance of books in the early stages of educating the deaf as "the chief lesson, I think, to be learned from the case of Helen Keller."

At the 1891 summer meeting of the American Association for the Promotion of the Teaching of Speech to the Deaf (also AAPTSD), an organization started the year before by Bell and some associates, Bell gave each member a copy of a handsomely bound "Helen Keller Souvenir." This book contained accounts of Helen's education by Annie Sullivan and others, among them Sarah Fuller, who had recently given Helen her first lessons in speech. At the Association's expense Helen and Miss Sullivan came in person to the 1893 meeting in Chicago, and Helen "saw" the World's Fair Exposition through the hands of Bell and her teacher; the tour included an exhibit of Bell's telephone. Teachers of the deaf met her and, it was reported, "saw and heard enough to remove all their doubts." A year later, at the AAPTSD Chautauqua meeting, Annie Sullivan delivered—or rather, out of last minute shyness, asked Bell to deliver for her—an eloquent yet objective account of her work and relations with Helen. And in 1896 the sixteen-year-old Helen herself proudly addressed the AAPTSD. "If you knew all the joy I feel in being able to speak to you today," she said, "I think you would have some idea of the value of speech to the deaf . . . One can never consent to creep when one feels an impulse to soar."

Helen Keller and Annie Sullivan were, however, much more to Bell than phenomena or specimens. They were his friends, and he was theirs. "It was an immense advantage for one of my temper, impatience, and antagonisms to know Dr. Bell intimately over a long period of time," said Annie in retrospect. "Gifted with a voice that itself suggested genius, he spoke the English language with a purity and charm which have never been surpassed by anyone I have heard speak. I listened to every word fascinated...I never felt at ease with anyone until I met him...Dr. Bell had a happy way of making people feel pleased with themselves. He had a remarkable faculty of bringing out the best that was in them. After a conversation with him I felt released, important, communicative. All the pent-up resentment within me went out...I learned more from him than from anyone else. He imparted knowledge with a beautiful courtesy that made one proud to sit at his feet and learn. He answered every question in the cool, clear light of reason...(with) no trace of animus against individuals, nations, or classes. If he wished to criticize, and he often did, he began by pointing out something good I had done in another direction." When asked long after Bell's death what, aside from her feeling for Helen, had enabled her to keep at so exacting a task for so many years, she replied, "I think it must have been Dr. Bell—his faith in me."

Bell's own daughters felt a touch of jealousy at his feeling for Helen Keller. For her part, one of her early letters, written a few months after teacher first came to her, was to "Dear Mr. Bell," and it said, among other things, "I do love you." And more than thirty years later, when he was seventy-one, she wrote him, "Even before my teacher came, you held out a warm hand to me in the dark...You followed step by step my teacher's efforts...When others doubted it, it was you who heartened us...You have always shown a father's joy in my successes and a father's tenderness when things have not gone right."

More than once in those thirty years things did go wrong for Helen Keller, and Bell was there with a helping hand. A short story, *The Frost King*, which she wrote in 1891 at the age of eleven for Anagnos' birthday and which Anagnos then published, was found to echo the plot and wording of a children's fairy tale published nearly twenty years earlier, a story unknown to Annie Sullivan and not in the books available to Helen. It turned out to have been read to her at the home of a friend in Annie's absence more than three years earlier. At the Perkins Institution a solemn committee (Mark Twain in his outrage called it "a collection of decayed human turnips") cross-questioned the bewildered and frightened child at great length, with Annie Sullivan sent out of the room, before concluding that Helen had unwittingly summoned up the story from her remarkable memory rather than from her imagination as she supposed. The ordeal crushed Helen's spirit and her joy in books for months and shook her confidence in her own originality for years.

The kindly author of the original story, Margaret Canby, wrote that Helen's version was no plagiarism but "a wonderful feat of memory" and "an improvement on the source." "Please give her my warm love," added Miss Canby, "and tell her not to feel troubled over it any more." Mark Twain was more emphatic, recalling the time he himself had unconsciously plagiarized a passage from Oliver Wendell Holmes. "To think of those solemn donkeys breaking a little girl's heart with their ignorant damned rubbish about plagiarism!" he wrote. "I couldn't sleep for blaspheming about it last night." Bell, who had helped Annie Sullivan trace Helen's exposure to the story, saw further than either Twain or Miss Canby. Like them, he pointed out that "we all do what Helen did," that "our most original compo-

Helen Keller, Annie Sullivan (standing), Alexander Graham Bell,
July 1894

sitions are composed exclusively of expressions derived from others." But he also observed that Anagnos had "failed to grasp the importance of the Frost King incident" and that a "full investigation will throw light on the manner in which Helen has acquired her marvelous knowledge of language— and do much good."

After a long talk with Helen in 1894 Bell heartily seconded her "strong desire" to be educated in a school for normal students rather than in a special school for the deaf or the blind. Bell reminded Captain Keller that his daughter would need a special interpreter in any case, so a school for the handicapped could offer her no practical advantage. He promised to rally Helen's friends to the underwriting of any expenses. Thus Helen went on to achieve what throughout her life would be one of her chief consolations and sources of pride: acceptance as an intellectual and social equal by people who could see and hear.

In 1897 Arthur Gilman, headmaster of the Cambridge School, at which Helen was preparing for Radcliffe College, decided that Miss Sullivan was endangering Helen's health by pressing too hard in her studies. Having temporarily persuaded Helen's mother of this, he tried to separate Helen from her beloved teacher. Gilman did his best to win Bell's support for the move. But Bell had boundless faith in the wisdom and dedication of Annie Sullivan, and when she appealed to him for help, he dispatched his assistant, the venerable John Hitz, to investigate. Afterward Bell wrote Gilman that nothing could justify parting Helen and Annie except evidence that Annie was in some way unfit for her charge; and as to that, his free conversation with Helen had revealed her to be a "living testimonial to the character of Miss Sullivan." Mrs. Keller hurried to Massachusetts and, finding Helen in excellent health and determined to stay with Annie, agreed with Hitz and Bell that Gilman was wrong. Never again was it to be suggested that Helen and Annie Sullivan should be parted.

Three years later, just as Helen entered Radcliffe College, a well-intentioned friend nearly persuaded her to give up her studies and, together with Annie, to start and direct a school for deaf-blind children. Bell's decided opposition to the scheme, along with that of other friends, kept Helen in Radcliffe and out of what would surely have been a fiasco.

Bell's doubts of his own business acumen led him to decline the suggestion that he administer a trust fund set up for Helen in 1896. Nevertheless, he took a leading part in organizing the arrangement and contributed a thousand dollars to it. Before and after, he helped out on special occasions, sending Helen four hundred dollars when her father died in 1896, a hundred dollars toward a country vacation in the summer of 1899, $194 so that Helen could surprise Annie with a wedding gift when Annie married the writer and critic John A. Macy in 1905. Financial as well as moral support may have led Annie to write early in 1898 that Bell "will never know how deeply grateful I am to him for one of the richest and fullest years we have ever known."

Among Helen's friends and admirers were those who were richer than Bell and less deeply committed to the support of other causes. In dollar terms their gifts to Helen outstripped those of Bell. But he gave her things they could not match with money. "More than anyone else, during those (early) years," wrote a friend who knew Helen in later life, "it was Alexander Graham Bell who gave Helen her first conception of the progress of mankind, telling her as much about science as Phillips Brooks told her about religion." Bell thrilled her with stories that paralleled the Greek epics she loved, Promethean tales like that of the laying of the Atlantic cable. One day he placed her hand on a telephone pole and asked her what it meant to her, then explained that the wires it carried sang of life and death, war and finance, fear and joy, failure and success, that they pierced the barriers of space and touched mind to mind throughout the whole of the civilized world.

Bell's mind, and Helen's through his, responded to nature, too. Once, beneath an oak, he placed her hand on the trunk, and she felt the soft crepitation of raindrops on the leaves. For years after that she liked to touch trees in the rain. Then, on another day, he went with her to Niagara Falls and put her hand on the hotel windowpane so that she could sense the thunder of the river plunging over its shuddering escarpment. He drove with her and Annie from Washington into the springtime countryside, where they gathered wild azalea, honeysuckle, and dogwood blossoms.

More than once Helen visited Beinn Bhreagh, the Bells' summer estate in Nova Scotia. She spent one night with Bell's daughters Elsie and Daisy on their houseboat, from which they all climbed down by a rope ladder to swim in the moonlit lake. In the fields overlooking the Bras d'Or Lakes, Bell told her of his kite flying and his hopes of giving wings to mankind. "He makes you feel that if you only had a little more time, you, too, might be an inventor," she wrote. One windy day she helped him fly his kites. "On one of them I noticed that the strings were of wire, and having had some experience in bead work, I said I thought they would break. Dr. Bell said 'No!' with great confidence, and the kite was sent up. It began to pull and tug, and lo, the wires broke, and off went the great red dragon, and

Bell and Helen Keller flying a kite at Beinn Bhreagh

poor Dr. Bell stood looking forlornly after it. After that he asked me if the strings were all right and changed them at once when I answered in the negative. Altogether we had great fun." Back at Radcliffe that summer of 1901 she wrote Mabel that "the smell of the ocean, and the fragrance of the pines have followed me to Cambridge and linger about me like a benediction."

Now and then Bell thought about Helen's future course in life. As she made her way through college he began to feel that "with her gifts of mind and imagination there should be a great future open to her in literature." Later he wrote her, "You must not put me among those who think that 'nothing you have to say about the affairs of the universe would be interesting.'" But Helen was more realistic about the limits put upon her direct apprehension of the world, about her inescapable dependence on the words of others for learning what eyes and ears tell most people. She knew also that to the public her blindness was her foremost characteristic (though personally she agreed with Mabel Bell that deafness was the heavier cross), so her work came to be more and more that of helping the cause of the blind. And because Bell's work lay with the deaf, he and she saw less of each other as the new century wore on.

Each missed the other. When he tried his hand at a letter in Braille while she was in college, she praised him for not making a single mistake. "It seemed almost as if you clasped my hand in yours and spoke to me in the old, dear way," she wrote him. In 1907 he wrote her, "I often think of you and feel impelled to write but—as you know—I am a busy man, and... have always lots of back correspondence to make up." Now and then he wrote again in Braille, but not often enough for it to be easy. He spent a few days in Boston once and tried for a long time one day to telephone Helen's house, but Annie heard the ringing too late. "We seem bound every time to miss seeing him," Helen wrote John Hitz on that occasion. As public figures, each knew in a general way what the other was doing. "I suppose," wrote Helen in 1902, "Mr. Bell has nothing but kites and flying-machines on his tongue's end. Poor dear man, how I wish he would stop wearing himself out in this unprofitable way—at least it seems unprofitable to me." But six years later she sent him a note of congratulation on his successes in aviation, to which he replied in proud detail.

In January 1907, Helen wired Bell "I need you." She was to speak in New York at a meeting for the blind; but Annie, who usually repeated her speech for those who might have difficulty understanding Helen's voice, was sick. Bell left Washington at once and lent his matchless voice to the occasion.

In the summer of 1918 Helen asked Bell to play himself in a motion picture of her life. He was then seventy-one, in uncertain health, very susceptible to summer heat, and had "the greatest aversion to appearing in a moving-picture." Still, her letter touched him deeply. "It brings back recollections of the little girl I met in Washington so long ago," he wrote her. "You will," he reminded her, "have to find someone with dark hair to impersonate the Alexander Graham Bell of your childhood." But he promised to appear with her in a later scene, when the hot weather was over, if she wanted him to. To his great relief he was not called upon (which was just as well, since the film was a grotesque failure, both as drama and as history).

The drama of Helen Keller's rescue and rise had, after all, been given a far more enduring form in her own autobiography, *The Story of My Life*, fifteen years before. Supplemented by her own and Annie Sullivan's letters, it both recounted and attested to one of history's most moving triumphs. And it began with the words

To
Alexander Graham Bell
Who has taught the deaf to speak
and enabled the listening ear
to hear speech
from the Atlantic to the Rockies,
I dedicate
this Story of My Life.

Theodore N. Vail

3

Theodore N. Vail, Architect of the Bell System

The saying is that Alexander Graham Bell invented the telephone and Theodore Vail invented the telephone business. Who was this man? How did he fit into the puzzle? Why did Theodore Vail feel so strongly about the importance of customer service that he resigned at the age of 42 rather than compromise his principles? And how did it come to pass that he returned in triumph twenty years later to save the company he loved?

Much of the following is excerpted from the 1922 biography of Theodore Vail, *In One Man's Life*, by Albert Bigelow Paine. Mr. Paine also penned a highly regarded biography of Mark Twain, and his Hollow Tree stories for younger readers are still in print.

I. Background and Early Years

Theodore Vail's lineage has been traced back, with some degree of confidence, to 1647 and one Thomas Vail of Southampton, Long Island. Records show Thomas Vail owned a tract of land and was probably a farmer, although a portion of his time was given to "whale watching," which consisted of patrolling the beach to watch for cast-up whales. This was an important industry to those early settlers, who assembled at the first signal to secure the whale and divide up the valuable proceeds. His wife, Sarah, must have been a resolute person with a potent vocabulary for it is a matter of the record of that time that once, when defending herself in some debate, she used such masterful words that she was brought before a magistrate and sentenced to stand with her tongue in a cleft stick "so long as the offense committed by her was read and declared."

Thomas and Sarah Vail's descendants, who included Stephen Vail, eventually migrated to the Morristown area of New Jersey. Stephen Vail bought a forge in 1807 at the nearby town of Speedwell, which he enlarged and operated very successfully. It was at the Speedwell Iron Works in 1818 that the engines of the Savannah, the first steamship to cross the Atlantic, were begun.

Speedwell also manufactured important parts of the first American locomotives, and it was here in 1838 that Stephen Vail's son, Alfred, along with the inventor Samuel Morse, gave the first public demonstration of the electro-magnetic telegraph. Stephen Vail's money had made this demonstration possible, and it was Alfred Vail who developed Morse's idea, in time adding every device that made it practical including the dot and dash system of writing.

Theodore Newton Vail, the subject of this story, was born July 16, 1845, in Carroll County, Ohio, to Davis and Phebe Vail. His growing up years appear to have been quite average. Young Theo, or Doe as he was sometimes called, was mischievous and was no more than an average student. His penmanship, spelling, and English composition were very bad. He was a good mathematician, however, and was also very interested in chemistry, philosophy, and astronomy, reading all he could find on those subjects. Still, he was hardly a leader or even a promising boy. A relative once complained to Vail's father, "Davis, that boy is always whistling!"

Career Choices

As Vail advanced through high school he saw other boys starting at some trade or profession, but he could not make up his mind. He considered becoming a preacher, a lawyer, a doctor like his uncle, an explorer, or a scientist. When high school ended and he still had not decided, he took a job as a clerk in a drug store. There was a telegraph office in the drug store, which young Vail found much more interesting than dispensing medicines. Its scientific and mechanical aspects appealed to him, and its essence appealed to his

Theodore Vail at 16

romantic nature: a telegraph operator could go anywhere. Furthermore, the telegraph was a Vail tradition; the association of Alfred Vail in its invention and its development at the Speedwell Iron Works had brought honor to the family. He had heard the story time and again from his earliest childhood.

He remained in the drug store about two years, and at the end of that time knew a great deal more about telegraphy than of drugs. He had even made one or two magnetic instruments of his own and had learned to read messages if not sent too rapidly. After leaving the drug store he obtained a job as a telegraph operator with Western Union in New York, where he led the carefree life of a single young man out on his own for the first time.

In 1866, following the end of the American civil war, expansion to the West reached a fever pitch and Theodore Vail's family joined in. Theodore left the telegraph business to accompany them to the fertile wilderness of Iowa. They established a farm in the virgin Iowa prairie, near Waterloo, where in winter the temperature often fell to twenty degrees below zero.

The job of "busting" the eighty acres of sod fell to Theodore. It was exhausting work, stumbling behind a team of horses for long hours each day, but on the whole he enjoyed it. He always had a taste for conquest, and here was a new world to conquer. At night he returned to the house weary from work but with an appetite for food and sleep such as he had never known.

In 1867, after the harvest, he took a position as a teacher in a country school about three miles from the family home; he would maintain a strong interest in education and make significant contributions to it his entire life. He had begun to grow restless in Iowa, however, and in the spring of the following year, at age 23, he applied for and received a job as a telegraph operator with Union Pacific in the frontier location of Pinebluff, Wyoming. He had hardly reached the turning point of life but had begun to suspect its existence.

Vail in the Wild West

His reception in Pinebluff was not especially cheerful. On the railway platform lay a dead man; he had been killed by Indians the day before and was badly mutilated. The body lay in plain view, uncovered, and seemed to attract little attention as Indian attacks against the expansionists were quite common then. The railroad was at that time nearing completion, the work being performed by tough, warlike gangs of men who often required the protection of soldiers. Once, Theodore and his brother Alonzo, who had also moved to the area, found themselves facing a number of Indians while out on the mesa on horseback. The brothers wheeled their horses and made a dash for the town. A group of cavalry soldiers saw the race and came riding to the rescue, where one man was killed in the skirmish.

Doubtless the Indians were simply responding to what they correctly perceived as the invasion of their land by the white settlers. Trainloads of passengers arrived almost daily and Vail, with his natural gift for expansion, inaugurated changes in the Pinebluff telegraph office. Not content with the local wire service, he obtained approval for Pinebluff to become a testing station complete with two through wires; this put the remote office in direct touch with the affairs of the world. Such was the vision, action, and accomplishment that would characterize the long and productive life of Theodore Vail.

Vail Conquers the Postal Service

Vail was not to remain in Pinebluff for long. He was engaged to be married to Emma Righter of Newark, and he had no wish to bring a young, Eastern-bred girl to the hazards and hardships of the frontier. He wrote to an uncle who had influence in Washington, and received an appointment as a mail clerk in the U.S. Postal Railway System for the salary of nine hundred dollars a year. Vail and Emma were married on August 3, 1869. Vail's performance in his new job was excellent and in a short time he received a raise in wages to one thousand, then to twelve hundred dollars, the maximum for that position.

Vail achieved notoriety and rose rapidly through the ranks as a result of his developing a vastly improved system for the distribution of mail. The method of operation when he became a mail clerk on the Union Pacific Railroad was that, at each stop, the mail was dumped from its sacks, the mail for that stop removed, then all remaining mail put back into the sacks. At the next stop it was dumped out again and the process repeated, sometimes accurately and sometimes not. Letters were often weeks or even months on the road, arriving at their destination stained and travel worn.

Vail got into the habit of removing not only the mail for the Union Pacific stations but also for the small settlements reached only by stagecoach. He would then tie the letters for a particular destination into bundles, properly marked with a slip of paper in each, thus making it possible for the mails to

81

arrive a day, two days, even a week earlier at their destinations. He bought maps and marked out the connecting routes, memorizing the names of the towns on each.

Then it occurred to him that a chart conveying this information would be valuable and he constructed one, a simple scheme showing the connecting points and the names of the towns. He and his associates found it to be extremely helpful and began to take pride in sending the mail along in the quickest time and with the fewest mistakes. The stagecoaches at the distributing points no longer had to wait while sacks disgorged their mixed contents to be sorted and discussed by inefficient grocery clerks and bartenders doubling as mail clerks. The sacks contained only bundles, each properly tied and labeled, and the stages could be off at once. Vail and his companions had planted a seed that would grow into civil service reform.

As with many of the circumstances in the life of Theodore Vail, this seed was planted at the right time of the moon. George B. Armstrong of the Chicago Post Office, a pioneer in the advancement of the mail service, had in 1869 been appointed General Superintendent of the Railway Mail Service. He was determined to revolutionize the Railway Mail Service and began to ask around for new ideas. He learned of what Vail had done on the Union Pacific, and Vail was eventually selected for the run between Iowa City and Chicago, then later made chief clerk of the Iowa City run. Vail and his associates also made up distribution schemes for that route, realizing the same efficiencies as before.

When Armstrong retired two years later due to poor health he was succeeded by George S. Bangs, a tireless worker whose number one objective was to carry on the work Armstrong had begun. He soon learned it was Vail who had initiated schematic distribution in the West. In February 1873 Bangs promoted Vail to Washington, D.C. to expand his more efficient system into the vast network of rails throughout the United States.

Vail became obsessed with his mammoth project, which included long hours of studying and memorizing complicated railway maps in order to determine the most efficient means of mail handling and delivery; with only small exaggeration it may be said he thought of nothing else and talked of nothing else. As before, his efforts paid off. The project was a huge success, reducing delivery time from as long as several weeks to as short as two or three days. Vail was quickly promoted to second in command to Bangs.

Perhaps the finest tribute to Theodore Vail was that his successes were met with almost no resentment or jealousy, but rather an outpouring of sincere warmth and congratulations from admiring peers and co-workers. An example from this particular promotion is from J.B. Furay of Omaha, a former clerk who wrote, "Vail you have, as we all out here feel, faithfully *earned* the laurels won, and we hope to hear of your continued recognition, for we have faith that you belong by nature still further up the scale."

The promotion doubled his salary, to thirty-five hundred dollars a year, though it was still not enough. No salary would ever be enough for Theodore Vail, who all his life spent money with an open hand, or even both hands open. Frank Riblett, a friend, long afterward wrote, "His habit of lavish expenditure I never could understand. He seemed to act on the certainty that the money would always be forthcoming in due time. And it always was."

Vail was also instrumental in the conception and development of the Fast Mails, a line of trains exclusively for mail between New York and Chicago, stopping only at the important cities and covering the distance in approximately 24 hours. There were many critics who prophesied failure, but on September 17, 1875 the dream became reality.

Bangs retired later that year, and with the beginning of the new year, only weeks before Alexander Graham Bell and Thomas Watson's historic first sentence communicated over the telephone, Theodore N. Vail replaced Bangs to become General Superintendent of the Railway Mails. In the seven years since his first connection with the service he had progressed from the humblest place in the ranks to the highest position the department had to offer.

II. The Bell Company Before Theodore Vail

For the fledgling Bell company the invention of the telephone was only the beginning of a long and difficult struggle. Bell's patent application had been filed on February 14, 1876, and it was so revolutionary it was granted almost immediately, on March 3 (Bell's birthday), and issued on March 7. Bell and Watson had only begun demonstrating the telephone in public in the spring of 1876, where it was regarded with interest and amusement but hardly a thought as to commercial value. Many people didn't know what to think. Some considered it supernatural, something of the occult, not of this world and better kept out of it. One noted journalist later wrote, "I remember well my disgust when I first heard of the human voice being transmitted over wires."

It was Bell's demonstration of the telephone for Emperor Dom Pedro of Brazil at the U.S. Centennial Exposition of Philadelphia on April 20, 1876, that put the telephone on the map; incidentally, it was on that same date, 2,000 miles to the west, that General Custer and his men were earning a spot in history the hard way. The demand for demonstrations soared following publicity of the emperor's delight at the telephone, and Bell finally earned some money from his invention through the sale of admission tickets to those public showings.

Speech transmission over longer distances improved greatly that fall and winter, which was necessary to maintain a successful business venture. The first commercial wire, spanning the three miles from Charles Williams's machine shop (where Bell and Watson had met) to Williams's house, was opened on April 4, 1877.

Western Union Enters the Scene

It was around this time that the potential commercial value of the telephone became more evident. One year earlier the mighty Western Union telegraph company had turned down flat an opportunity to buy for a pittance all rights to the

Bell patents; now Western Union began opening its own telephone lines in direct defiance of those same patents in the
hopes of overturning them in court.

Dark Days and a White Knight

It is difficult for us today to comprehend how financially frail the embryonic Bell company was, or how uncertain its
future. Imagine the burden of the nearly hopeless odds faced
by the fledgling company, consisting only of Hubbard, Sanders,
Watson, and Bell. In late 1877 Watson was occupied with tech-
nical issues and Bell had sailed for England to introduce the
telephone to Europe, but it was Sanders and Hubbard—primarily Sanders—whose every nickel in the world was on the
line. They extended everything they had, and then some, and
then some more, until they were stretched to the breaking
point. In Western Union they now faced a ruthless adversary
of unlimited financial and legal backing, bent on crushing them
with no thought of compromise.

On February 22, 1878, Sanders wrote, "How on earth
can we make our position better when we have nothing more
to fight with?" Hubbard and Sanders finally agreed to a plan to
attempt to raise money by the sale of stock, which is where
Theodore Vail entered the scene to become a part of telephone
history.

Vail was already familiar with the telephone and its possibilities first hand. He knew Gardiner Hubbard well, for
Hubbard was a member of a Congressional Postal Committee
which had made a tour of inspection with Vail officially in
charge. Hubbard carried his pair of telephones with him, and
was continuously experimenting. It was just the sort of thing
to appeal to Theodore Vail, who had always been intensely
interested in ideas for patents that would revolutionize the
world. Telegraphy, the Vail tradition, paled in comparison to
the potential of talking by wire. Hubbard had a pair of the
instruments sent to Vail's house.

Vail with his inventive mind and passion for improvements saw that the machine, perfected, would revolutionize

the world of speech. He pledged himself to take all the stock he could raise money to pay for. Returning to Washington he began moving heaven and earth to raise funds. He borrowed as he had never borrowed before, pledging whatever securities creditors were willing to take, urging friends to follow his example.

Hubbard, who had admired Vail from the start, had begun soon after meeting him to discuss with him the possibility of taking a position with the Bell company. Nothing could have appealed more to Vail's mind. He hesitated only because he had a young son in addition to his wife and felt he needed a reasonably certain income. As the months passed and the demand for telephones increased, Hubbard painted the prospects brighter and brighter, and Vail was increasingly tempted to cast his lot with the Bell forces. When the Western Union fight developed he was tempted still more. The injustice of the attack on the feeble corporation placed him squarely on the side of the underdog.

It was bureaucratic haggling over trivia that brought him at last to decision, a discussion in Congress that lasted an entire day's session as to continuation of Vail's five dollar a day expense allowance in addition to his salary. It was not a question as to whether the money was deserved, but the fact that distinguished senators should wrangle for a whole day over such a petty matter was discouraging; it made him realize the futility of any hope for advancement in a position where politics were involved.

Vail told Hubbard he was ready to leave government service, and that he didn't care what title he had as long as it was a job where there was the chance his work would count for something. He was assured it would be that kind of a job, and it was agreed his title would be general manager of the company. On June 2, 1878, Hubbard's secretary wrote to Sanders, "Mr. Vail has finally and fully determined to cast his lot with you. I am sure you will like Mr. Vail and his way of doing business."

In a letter to Vail at this time, Hubbard wrote, "We rely upon your executive ability, your fidelity, and unremitting zeal."

Vail replied, "My faith in the success of the enterprise is such that I am willing to trust to it, and I have confidence that we shall establish the harmony and cooperation essential to the success of an enterprise of this kind."

News of Vail's resignation had a huge reaction in the government. There was both concern that he was throwing away a secure position on such a shaky enterprise, especially with the Western Union lawsuit pending, and regret at losing such a valuable manager. A congressman wrote, "Can't you wait and see if Congress will not fix your salary? Don't rob the public of an invaluable servant just because we tried to cheat and starve you."

Theodore Vail was thirty-three years old, at his physical and mental best, and fairly surging with energy and enthusiasm. He would need all of it, and then some.

III. New Beginnings

Hubbard had promised Vail the New York telephone franchise as an added inducement to employment, and Vail had begun the formation of the New York Telephone company while still in Washington. Realizing that if any telephone franchise was valuable it was that of New York City, Vail assembled his friends and formed the company. One thousand fifty shares were issued, with Vail having 150.

The franchise contract between New York Telephone and the Bell parent became an example to be followed in the thousands of cities and towns between the eastern and western oceans. In potential wealth it was one of the richest contracts ever drawn.

The establishment of New York Telephone is significant because it represents the general model by which it was proposed to extend the telephone industry. The Bell company had no capital to construct a general telephone system; it could hardly afford to build the telephones themselves to supply orders. Vail and his associates realized there was just one way to carry out the work: local companies must be promoted in the various towns, the stock to be locally subscribed, a percentage to go to the Bell company for the franchise with a rental charge for the use of the instruments. It was a big idea—even if simple in theory—one of the biggest ever conceived; putting it into operation was another matter.

Rarely has there been such chaos of business affairs as Theodore Vail found when he took his new job. A good deal had been done, but most of it had been done wrong. Energetic employees had been running around in circles trying to create a mighty industry with no precedent to follow, no directing hand, no capital, nothing but a patent and such funds as had been scraped together by Thomas Sanders, a manufacturer of shoe soles.

With bankruptcy an ever-present menace, an impending lawsuit against a corporation of limitless capital, with nothing to go on but backbone, a genius for organization, a serene faith in the future and in himself, Theodore Vail undertook his giant task.

Getting Organized

With the New York company established, the next requirement was an organization for the functioning and management of the system. On July 20, 1878, the reorganization of the Bell Telephone Company, with a capital of $450,000, was completed. The new officers were Gardiner Hubbard, president; Thomas Sanders, treasurer; Alexander Graham Bell, electrician; Thomas A. Watson, general superintendent; and Theodore N. Vail, general manager and the only salaried officer at the time.

Preparing for Battle

One of the first tasks Vail performed was to send out a copy of Bell's patents to Bell agents in different parts of the country, urging them to stick to their guns in the face of Western Union's direct violation of those patents.

"We have the original telephone patents," he wrote, "we have organized and introduced the business, and we do not propose to have it taken from us by any corporation." He went on to say, "Professor Alexander Graham Bell has been adjudged the inventor of the speaking telephone by every scientific body that has considered the question, and it is believed that the opinion of the courts will give legal confirmation of this great moral judgment."

Having reassured and encouraged existing Bell companies, capable and energetic agents were sent out to establish new ones. In nearly every town it was possible to find some ambitious young person who was willing to interest fellow townspeople in setting up a telephone exchange. Further, those who had a telephone installed were often willing to become stockholders.

Contracts made with local companies in towns of whatever size were similar to that made by New York Telephone. While this sowed the seeds for future prosperity it actually increased the financial burden in the short term; the telephones were costly to make and their low monthly rental did not cover expenses. Williams's manufacturing company bore much of this burden as it was impossible to get money fast enough to cover payroll and the cost of materials. Williams had already been obliged to take stock as partial payment, stock that was then of questionable value. These were hard, discouraging days.

The Eternal Optimist

Manager Vail, it seemed, was not in the least dismayed by the prospects. He worked as if he had infinite resources of capital as well as courage. He laid out his campaign on a large scale and constantly introduced new features, among them a five year standard contract which required the local companies to build exchanges and confined them to certain areas.

There were also contracts which provided for connecting two or more towns, though there was little call for these. How could the telephone ever be made to work at any distance when often it refused to be heard across the street?

Vail, however, never doubted for a minute this possibility and planned accordingly. In his vision he saw interlinking wires extending from city to city and across the states, and even began securing interstate rights. His plan was to create a national telephone system in which the Bell company would be a permanent partner. He was undoubtedly already forming the philosophy behind his later slogan: "One policy, one system, universal service."

Paying the Price

Vail and his management team worked early and late, seven days a week. Outwardly at least, results began to show. The popularity of the telephone grew tremendously. Local companies multiplied; the demand for telephones increased beyond the limits of the Bell company to manufacture, and even further beyond its ability to pay for them. The company was constantly on the verge of bankruptcy through its prosperity.

Further, the actual workings of the telephone instruments and the fledgling networks were far from trouble-free. The telephone was still comparatively crude, conversations through it often being full of sound and fury. In most cases the ground wire was also used for the return circuit, an arrangement that was by no means satisfactory. The wires themselves, being of iron and poorly insulated, were only a degree better. In the towns they were generally paralleled by telegraph and other circuits which, through induction, added to the distracting noises that resembled a more or less continuous accompaniment of fireworks.

The Carbon Test

The transmitter, too, was still primitive, more calculated to "develop the voice and lungs than to promote conversation," in the words of Watson himself. When Thomas Edison developed the carbon transmitter for Western Union, superior in every way to that in use by Bell, near-panic gripped the offices of the Bell company.

Herbert Casson, in *The History of the Telephone,* characterized the situation this way: "Lessees of Bell telephones clamored with one voice for a transmitter as good as Edison's. This, of course, could not be had in a moment, and the five months that followed were the darkest days in the childhood of the telephone. How to compete with Western Union, which had this superior transmitter, a host of agents, a network of wires, millions of dollars of capital—that was the immediate problem that confronted the new general manager . . . several of his captains deserted, and he was then compelled to take control of their unprofitable exchanges as well. There was scarcely a mail delivery that did not bring him some bulletin of discouragement or defeat."

Temptation always comes at such times. Watson was offered $10,000 for his stock, Vail was tendered positions with higher and surer salary by railroad and express companies, and Sanders was urged to go back to his leather business, which had all but expired. But still they kept on.

Confidence and Serenity

Vail's calmness during these trying days was an invaluable asset. Members of the force, dismayed at the financial situation and at the powers lined up against them, would look over at him sitting at his desk, serene, undisturbed, quietly writing, and take courage.

A story that captures the essence of Vail's disposition was told by an assistant named Devonshire, who described the new general manager's first visit to the Boston office: "After greetings were over he sat down, placing his hat on the sill of the window. He was in an awkward position, and accidentally knocked his hat out of the window into the open alley two stories below. We did not expect to get it back again, or if we did we assumed its usefulness would be gone, but when recovered it was found to be uninjured. Regardless, its possible loss did not seem to faze Mr. Vail in the slightest."

Devonshire made up his mind that nothing could disturb Vail. He could even, while writing, steadily carry on an

Vail in 1879

almost continuous conversation. Associates noticed, too, that he never seemed to have the least misgivings as to the future. He planned for it, but always as if it were a certainty. He crossed no bridges till he came to them, and then always with a confidence that sustained those around him. Once long afterward when he spoke of that time he was asked, "Didn't you ever get discouraged?"

"If I did," Vail replied, "I never let anybody know it."

The Blake Transmitter to the Rescue

It was at the moment when conditions seemed most desperate that Francis Blake, Jr. of Boston informed the Bell company he had invented a transmitter as good as Edison's, or better, and agreed to let them have it in exchange for stock in the company. No single piece of news was ever more welcome to a struggling corporation. Blake's transmitter was all that he claimed and was put into use by the autumn of 1878.

We'll See You in Court

Many smaller companies in addition to Western Union were now operating telephone exchanges in violation of the Bell patents. Revitalized by the Blake transmitter, the Bell company brought suit against Peter A. Dowd of Boston, head of the American Speaking Telephone Company, for patent infringement. This was the first of what would eventually total more than 600 legal battles over Bell's original patents. Five of these cases would be decided by the highest court in the land, and all would result in victory for Bell.

In the case of Dowd, the Bell company had secured as its attorneys Chauncey Smith and James J. Storrow, men at the head of their profession and with the cause of the struggling company at heart. The strategy was to first obtain a decision in court against a foe of considerably less legal muscle than Western Union. The celebrated "Dowd case" lasted more than a year, then suddenly ended with complete victory for Bell.

Western Union Folds

George Gifford, chief attorney for Western Union, reported to his clients in May of 1879 that Alexander Graham Bell was the original inventor of the telephone. He suggested they withdraw their claims and make the best settlement they could.

Following his advice, Western Union offered to leave the local business to Bell and take for themselves the interexchange, or toll lines. Many in the Bell company were in favor of accepting this proposition, but Vail opposed it. Long distance telephoning was his ultimate goal and he had the fullest faith in its future.

A Settlement is Reached

The opposing forces finally met in New York and spent the better part of a night discussing disputed points. Around daybreak a basis of settlement was reached which permitted

Western Union to use and sublet telephones under license from Bell on their private wires, which was a small concession for Bell.

The whole matter was concluded the next day, November 10, 1879, on the following terms: Western Union agreed that Alexander Graham Bell was the inventor of the telephone, that his patents were valid, and that they would retire from the telephone business. The Bell company agreed to buy the telephones and telephone system of the Western Union, to pay it a royalty of twenty per cent of receipts from telephone rentals or royalties, and to keep out of the telegraph business.

The agreement was to remain in force for seventeen years, and was a triumph of Theodore Vail's policy of taking the enemy into camp. By it a giant competitor and bitter enemy was transformed into a partner and friend. It also added to the Bell System fifty-six thousand telephones in fifty-five cities around the United States. The way was cleared for prosperity at last.

The Corporation Takes Shape

By the time of the Western Union settlement the Bell Telephone Company had become the National Bell Telephone Company, with William H. Forbes, a son-in-law of Ralph Waldo Emerson, as president. Vail still held the position of general manager, and he and his staff moved from New York to 95 Milk Street in Boston. The telephone business was not entirely well of its financial infirmities, but it was highly convalescent.

At this point begins a great period in telephone history. For the first time there was money to work with and employees to do the work. Everybody, it seemed, wanted a telephone now. Telephone equipment could not be constructed fast enough to supply the demand and two or three other companies were permitted to make bells and switchboards.

The Rewards of Perseverance

With the Bell victory in the Dowd case it had begun to be evident to the public that Western Union had the weak side of the argument, and that the telephone was to take its place with the railroad and the telegraph as a world institution. Bell stock, which had started at $50 a share, had reached $350 by September. On November 11, when it became known that Bell and Western Union were to combine forces, it soared to $1,000 a share.

Gardiner Hubbard's dreams were realized; he and his associates were undeniably rich now. Vail was also in good position, but his fortunes were to be greatly increased by the end of the year, when National Bell purchased the stock of New York Telephone, in which Vail had steadily increased his holdings. He was, at age 35, a millionaire, recognized as the chief figure of the flourishing telephone industry, its managing head, having arrived at a place of power and responsibility few will ever know.

IV. Vail and Early Prosperity

In June 1881 Vail bought a house in Boston befitting his means and position, the big Chadwick house and grounds on Walnut Avenue, for more than fifty thousand dollars. It was a house of the period, American mid-Victorian, square and Mansard on the outside, square and Eastlake on the inside. The rooms were large, the grounds shady and ample.

Vail proceeded to expand and glorify it in his lavish way. When he finished there were gardens and greenhouses and stables, a fountain and wide sloping lawns. Inside were rich carpets and draperies, and prismed chandeliers. There were paintings that in time would fill the walls, statuary of bronze and marble in many corners. There was a billiard room, a wine cellar—everything, in short, that went to make up the home of wealth and luxury in that more exuberant day. Theodore Vail could only do things in a big way, from his homes to his great industrial achievements.

He was fond of animals and acquired some fine dogs and high-bred horses. The skill earlier acquired in directing those three horses hitched to a big prairie plow in Iowa qualified him to handle with confidence four handsome Kentucky greys; driving "four-in-hand" became his favorite diversion.

Technology Marches On

A matter of primary importance continued to be the improvement of telephone technology, which has continued since the day Watson made the first telephone with his own hands. Increasing the distance of conversations ever further was also a high priority, as was placing wires underground, especially in the larger cities.

Vail himself frequently suggested something new, and by 1882 had taken out a dozen patents; five were on signaling apparatus, three on circuit-closing devices, three on switchboards, and one on subterranean conductors.

Copper Wire

The immediate problem with longer distance was the wires. Iron wire has poor transmission qualities, but it is strong and durable. Copper wire was superior for transmission, but copper lines sagged in hot weather yet failed to contract in cold weather; they soon became useless, stretched-out things that sometimes touched the ground.

The solution to this problem was given a great boost with the discovery by Thomas Doolittle (who later helped found the Telephone Pioneers of America) that copper wire, drawn cold, acquires a degree of hardness and strength far superior to copper drawn the traditional way. By the spring of 1884, using cold drawn copper, a telephone conversation in which Vail participated had been accomplished between Boston and New York.

For Whom the Telephone Rings

With early telephone sets the only way to signal the other end that someone was trying to call was to tap lightly with a fingernail or a lead pencil on the diaphragm; this produced a slight clicking sound at the other end. It was Watson who developed the first signaling device, evolving it from a small hammer to take the place of the lead pencil, then a kind of buzzer (a relic of the harmonic telegraph), then a magneto-electric call-bell. The bell did not always work but was a great improvement. Once perfected it continued in use for many years.

Carty Conquers Conduction

The conduction problem remained troublesome. The ground wire was also used for the return circuit, which facilitated all sorts of extraneous noise. Blake's transmitter had helped, but interfering currents from parallel wires carrying telegraph, burglar alarm, and the new high-power electric-light voltage, often made conversation nearly impossible.

There was a young man waiting in the wings of the Boston exchange, however, who would one day become the chief engineer of the Bell System. His name was John J. Carty, and he had started as a youthful operator. It occurred to young Carty one day to double the wires rather than depending on the ground wire for the return circuit. He made the experiment with almost magical results, and clear, static-free conversations made their long-awaited and much-welcomed arrival on the scene.

A Philosophical Rift Appears

Growth continued steadily, with the 1885 annual report boasting dividends of more than a million and a half dollars paid from a return of less than three million dollars. In later years Theodore Vail admitted that a growing dissatisfaction with his position at this period was due in part to the compa-

Vail in 1885

ny's reluctance to spend money in keeping the service the best it could be, preferring to distribute larger dividends. It was this growing philosophical difference that led to the end of Vail's first turn at the helm in just two short years following.

AT&T Is Formed

The historic formation of the American Telephone and Telegraph Company was also announced in the 1885 report, along with the news that Vail would resign his position as general manager of the Bell company in order to assume the presidency of the new company, AT&T. There seems to have been a great deal of concern over Vail's health, created by evidence that the demanding duties of the job were proving a strain. Vail always seemed calm, even serene, although he sometimes had trouble sleeping. And, though he carried it well, his weight was definitely on the rise.

Speedwell Farms

In 1883, while paying a visit to the snowy Vermont hills, Vail fell in love with the area overlooking Lyndonville. He slept that night in the home of a friend and the next morning declared it the best night's sleep he had had in years. He arranged to buy an adjoining 250 acre farm even before returning to Boston, and immediately began preparations to send up a variety of articles that would add to its comforts.

He called it Speedwell Farms, carrying on the name associated with the family's Speedwell Iron Works. He stocked

Speedwell Farms

it with horses and cattle, added to the house and barns, and showed his interest in the community by donating two thousand dollars to the local high school, which had been closed for lack of funds. He returned each summer to Speedwell, and for respites in between, and the place grew and improved accordingly.

He entertained lavishly, sparing no expense to ensure the comfort and enjoyment of his guests. His annual birthday party, held at Speedwell each July 16, was a full-blown gala. He loved the place and would love it all his life.

Vail Resigns

He found Speedwell the perfect haven for rejuvenation when he resigned from his beloved telephone business due to failing health and the escalating controversy over service improvements versus short-term financial gain. The date was September 19, 1887; Theodore Vail was 42 years old.

Life Outside the Telephone Company

A complicating factor for Vail in deciding whether to resign was the swift erosion of the wealth he had earned from his telephone holdings. A series of bad investments plus the expensive upkeep on the estate in Boston had drained him financially. He sold the big house in Boston, moving to Speedwell full time.

In 1889 fate smiled on him again when an old Colorado mine he owned but had long since given up as hopeless began to pay. A new and richer vein of ore had been discovered and the money came tumbling in once again. Vail and his wife sailed for the Mediterranean to spend the winter, languishing in Europe for nearly two years. When they returned Vail's health was greatly improved.

He then settled into the life of a gentleman farmer, making constant improvements and expansions of Speedwell until it reached 2,500 acres. Additions and enhancements had been made to the house until it was an endless, rambling place, but still with the air of warmth and hospitality Vail always provided for his guests.

South American Ventures

One of those guests in the summer of 1894 was Walter Davis, an American astronomer in charge of the weather bureau of Cordoba, in the Argentine Republic. From boyhood Vail had been interested in South America; stories of the exploration of unknown rivers, of the endless stretches of waving pampa, the vast herds of native cattle, the snow-capped Andes, had stimulated his imagination and held him fascinated. Early in his telephone career he had established companies on the West Coast of Brazil but had never found time to visit. He listened eagerly when Davis told him of Cordoba, called the Athens of the Argentine—its oldest city, with Moorish architecture, plazas, and narrow streets, like a city of ancient Spain. He wanted to go there, and when Davis told him that at Cordoba was one of the greatest opportunities for electrical development by water power, he agreed almost on the spot to go down during the winter and engage in this great new enterprise.

Vail spent the better part of the next two years with this mammoth engineering project, spending the winters in Argentina and the summers at Speedwell. Long afterward he wrote, "There was never anything that quite took hold of my imagination as Cordoba did. We built a long house, the lower part of which was arranged for the manager of the station and the upper part for those who came from Cordoba to visit the place. We kept a very good native cook there, and had room for a few guests. When we got the dynamo in place the sound of it seemed a fitting accompaniment to the scenery. I never hear today the hum of an electrical machine that my mind doesn't instantly revert to those long beautiful nights, with a stillness unbroken except by the purr of the dynamo from the station."

While en-route on his first visit to the Argentine Vail had also met a man involved in a project to develop electric tram lines, and Vail became a partner in that undertaking also. Both ventures yielded profitable returns, and within a comparatively brief time Theodore Vail's South American developments had set him more firmly than ever on his financial feet and given him new prestige in the industrial world.

Personal Tragedies

In spite of his business successes the period 1905-1906 brought personal tragedy to Vail. His wife died suddenly on February 3, 1905, while Vail was in England. His son and only child Davis died December 20, 1906, while Vail was again overseas. His household now consisted of his widowed sister, Louise Brainard, and his niece, Katherine Vail. Following the death of his wife and son Vail seemed to be adrift, without plans for the future. The South American work no longer required his supervision; the farm was not enough to command his energies. He did consider politics, which had been one of his earlier ambitions, but his experiences with the political process from his Railway Mail days had soured him in that direction.

Prophecies of Late-Blooming Greatness

Five years before, in Paris, a fortune teller had assured Vail his greatest work would come after he was sixty, a prophecy repeated by a fortune teller in London. He had taken little stock in these predictions, and there seemed slight promise now of their fulfillment. Certainly he did not imagine his destiny was about to be realized.

AT&T Without Vail

A primary cause of Vail's resignation from AT&T had been conflict over his desire to channel more of the profits back into the improvement of service. With Vail's resignation the company's direction and its commitment to customer service had suffered greatly. Many in the company had viewed their mission as being to milk the Bell patents for all they were worth until their expiration. In Vail's absence the attitude of the company had become one of an elitist monopoly doing the public a favor; when the patents expired and the Bell company was no longer a monopoly, but continued to act as if it were, this was when the trouble really started.

With the expiration of Bell's patents in 1893 came a tremendous increase in independent companies, many in smaller towns and on farmer's lines where the Bell company had not established service and where there was no direct competition. Many were also directly competing in the same cities as the Bell franchises, ushering in the confusing, chaotic era of two or even three phone companies in the same city.

Vail Returns

By 1907 Vail had disposed of his South American interests. He had acquired great prestige as a director of large affairs, with important financial connections abroad. He had gradually increased his telephone holdings and even received a position on the board of AT&T. Several bankers heavily involved with the business, including J.P. Morgan, recommended making Vail president. Vail had already been asked to resume the presidency once before, in 1900, but his critical involvement in Argentina and the demands on his time were then so great that he refused.

Now, incredibly, at age 62 Vail was again being offered the highest position in the company he most loved. His sister, still at the head of his household, thought that he had had enough of business and urged him to decline. He answered, "No, I must take it. I refused it six years ago, but I'm in a position to take it now. Besides, they need me now."

A week later, on May 1, 1907, his election as president of the American Telephone and Telegraph Company was announced. The prophesied era of his greatest work had begun.

V. The Genius at Work

One of the first challenges Vail faced was one of finances. The company's bankers had a sizable supply of bonds they could not sell from the last offering and were running short of patience. "Don't worry," Vail reportedly told the bankers. "You will get rid of those and want more before the year is out."

Doubtless his claim sounded brash. Telephone stock had been declining steadily, along with other public securities, but president Vail knew public confidence in the telephone business was still unshaken. At the end of May he announced a stock issue of 220,000 shares, to be distributed among existing stockholders; each owner of six of the old shares would be entitled to purchase one of the new shares at par.

To the amazement of his associates the issue proved an astonishing success. More than two hundred thousand shares of the new stock were absorbed almost immediately. Rights for their purchase sold at a premium, and over twenty million dollars in cash was raised.

The net result went much further. Four months later, when the country's financial structure broke down in one of the worst panics in history—when trust companies, banks, and industrial corporations were closing their doors—the telephone company's credit remained unshaken.

Hard Choices

The financial problem had not been the only one that confronted the new president. To bring order out of the executive and manufacturing confusion, a drastic policy of retrenchment was inaugurated.

At Western Electric the indiscriminate and wasteful manufacture of equipment came to an end with the result that twelve thousand employees were let go. Engineering, which had become huge, scattered, unorganized, and redundant, also received prompt attention. Vail concentrated them all into Western Electric and divided Western Electric into three groups—at Chicago, Boston, and New York. John J. Carty, whose contributions had not ended with the discovery of double wire, presided over all of it as chief engineer. This was the seed group that in January 1925 would officially become the unparalleled pinnacle of technological development, Bell Laboratories.

Team Building

President Vail realized the necessity of making the personal acquaintance of his lieutenants, the heads of the associated companies, and their chief officials. During that first active summer of his return he chartered a yacht, the Mohican, and in small groups invited the prominent telephone officials of the country to cruise with him. He gave them trips up the Hudson and along the Sound, listened to their problems, entertained them in his regal fashion, and made their acquaintance in a way that insured close cooperation and friendship.

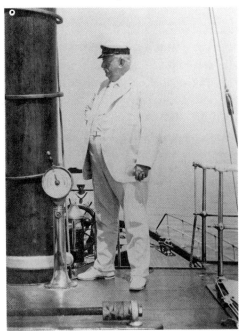

Vail on his yacht

Considered from the standpoint of later results, this was about the most important accomplishment of that first

busy season for this captain of organization, finance and diplomacy, who had now arrived at the place for which all the years
had prepared him. One might suppose he had been over-
whelmed by the responsibilities and burdens suddenly heaped
on him. Nothing of the sort; to those around him he seemed to
be taking matters quite easily, unhurried and unworried and
not greatly pressed for time.

He even had time to expand and improve Speedwell.
He bought four more farms that summer and added a tower to
Speedwell in honor of his new position. More than that, he
found time to get married again, this time to Mabel Sanderson
of Boston, on July 27, 1907. Truly it was an eventful year.

My, How You've Grown

During the twenty years of his absence the telephone
business had become like a new world, unbelievably vast in its
proportions. Its wires had multiplied more than thirty times, to
a grand total of eight and a half million miles, nearly half of
which was underground. Subscribers now totaled three million, a larger number having been added in the past year than
there had been in the entire country twenty years before. Vail
had left the industry in its lusty youth; he found it now a great
and wallowing giant, needing only to be set on its feet. As in
the beginning, it had turned to him in its hour of need, and the
new president believed the first thing it needed was a clear
sense of purpose, of mission.

Purpose and Conscience

He helped define the company's objective with a clear
sense of public conscience as well as corporate responsibility,
which he saw as mutually dependent rather than contradictory.
He also believed in stating things as clearly as possible, and
hated slick-packaged double-speak. His first annual report,
dated December 31, 1907, was characteristic of his frankness—
too much so, some of his directors were inclined to believe.
When it was mildly suggested that certain items might be

advantageously omitted, Vail said, "No, we will lay our cards on the table; there is never anything to be gained in the long run by concealment."

In *Telephone: the First Hundred Years,* John Brooks describes Vail's approach this way:

> Vail's presidential essays in AT&T annual reports are like nothing else in American business literature, before or since. They are personal, revealing, discursive, sometimes pontifical. "If we don't tell the truth about ourselves, some one else will," Vail said in 1911—reversing the secretive attitude of management that was the traditional and accepted one of the time—and in telling his version of the truth to stockholders in the annual reports, Vail thought nothing of running on for twenty or thirty pages. However, close perusal of those pages was usually rewarding.
>
> In his first and perhaps most famous annual essay, that for 1907, he led off with a section entitled *Public Relations*—by which, as the context made clear, he meant not advertising and promotion, but the whole scope of relations between the corporation and the public. For two decades, it is fair to say, the corporation had in a pinch put the welfare of its stockholders first and that of its customers, the telephone users, second. Public Relations in the Vail sense had therefore been defensive, designed to keep customer dissatisfaction within manageable bounds and to forestall drastic government action.
>
> Now Vail introduced the concept—all but new to American industry, and indeed outright heresy to its leading thinkers then—that maximum profit was not necessarily the *primary* objective of private enterprise. Profit was necessary to ensure the financial health that made possible renovation and innovation of facilities; but it was only one element in an equation. The problem was to achieve a proper balance. It was a new concept of the corporation.

Innovations and Milestones

Vail's second turn at the helm saw far too many highlights and milestones to mention here. Rapid advancements in technology, tremendous growth of the telephone network, and political upheaval around the world necessitated constant innovation in industrial method, salary and working conditions, and structure. Here is but a small sample of major accomplishments under Vail the second time around:

Pensions He initiated a pension plan that was entirely ahead of its time and is the model still in use by many companies today. Remembering his own hard-up times, he instituted a loan program wherein an employee could get up to a month's advance on his or her salary.

World War I Vail saw the company through the great World War, during which ownership passed to the federal government for the only time in history. Under government ownership efficiency plummeted, however, and when the U.S. entered World War II the issue of again transferring ownership to the government did not even come up.

Telephone Pioneers of America His support played a large role in the founding of the Telephone Pioneers of America. Vail was elected the first president of the Pioneers and re-elected president every year until his death.

Structure of the Operating Companies The Bell System had collected a nearly unmanageable number of diverse local companies. In 1911 Vail announced a consolidation of them into a much smaller number of state and regional companies, thus laying out the geographical lines of the Bell companies that lasted nearly intact until January 1, 1984.

Transcontinental Talk Vail helped create and was a listener in the first transcontinental telephone conversation. Previously, the "thousand mile talk" between New York and Chicago had been regarded as the practical limit for speech communication. This barrier was shattered thanks to innovations such as the loading coil, invented by Dr. Michael Pupin of Columbia University. Also contributing was the three element vacuum tube, developed by Harry D. Arnold, a Western

Theodore Vail and Alexander Graham Bell meet for the first time in thirty years. Directly behind Bell is Tom Watson

Electric scientist, and Dr. Lee de Forest, an inventor from outside the Bell System.

On January 25, 1915, the first words heard between the
coasts were from Alexander Graham Bell in New York to
Thomas Watson in San Francisco. Also on the hook-up were
President Woodrow Wilson in Washington and Vail from Jekyl
Island, Georgia, where he was recovering from a leg injury.

"Mr. Watson," Bell said, speaking through the original
instrument Watson had crafted by hand 39 years earlier,
"please come here. I want to see you."

"I should be happy to," Watson replied, "but now it
would take me a week instead of a minute."

Breathing New Life into Western Union

Vail, who believed strongly in the benefits of legitimate
natural monopolies, pushed further in this direction by becoming president of Western Union in 1909 while retaining his
duties with AT&T, which had acquired a sizable interest in the
telegraph company. Western Union was in serious trouble
then, having been nearly put out of business by the very telephone industry it once could have bought for $100,000. Vail
had always retained a fondness for the telegraph business and
saw the two forms of communication as complementary, natural auxiliaries.

The first thing he did was to clean up the dingy telegraph offices. Polished oak and shining plate glass began to
replace the smeary windows, rickety desks and counters;
bright new paint gave cheer and invitation to walls and ceil-
ings. Courtesy and prompt attention were stimulated by
increases in what had become paltry salaries.

Telegraph business picked up immediately. When telephone subscribers learned they could merely call a courteous
representative at Western Union, send a telegram and have it
charged to their telephone accounts, the public realized something dramatic had happened at Western Union. Business grew
rapidly, showing an increase of five million dollars at the end
of the first year.

Vail improved on a number of other conditions at Western Union, including taking advantage of slow periods for greater economy. He devised the night and day rated letters, the cable letter, and the weekend letter, all of which became very profitable. With the increased earnings the offices became still more attractive and more inviting, and further advancements in wages were allowed. By the end of the third year the pay of operators had increased a full fifty percent.

In an article in *Printer's Ink*, Charles W. Hurd wrote, "All that Theodore N. Vail did to Western Union . . . was to put life and courage into the demoralized force, improve the 25,000 telegraph offices scattered over the country, create several new telegraph and cable services to fill in the force's idle time, reduce the general cost to the public, and educate the latter to these new services and economies through country-wide advertising . . . only, nobody in the old organization had seen it before, had been aware of the real basic trouble, or knew where to begin to overcome it."

It was at about this time, however, that the long nose of the government arrived. The Department of Justice decided the association of the two companies violated the antitrust laws and required their separation. In 1913 the Western Union stock owned by the telephone company was disposed of, and Vail resigned the presidency of Western Union.

Regulatory Philosophy

In *Telephone: The First Hundred Years*, John Brooks also provides a summary of Vail's philosophy and approach toward regulation:

Vail astounded stockholders and colleagues by saying he had "no serious objection" to public control over telephone rates in the 1907 AT&T annual report. Over the following years his philosophy in regard to the proper relation between the telephone industry and the government evolved into what would become and remain for many years the accepted view of both industry and the government, that of a natural monopoly. Rejecting the old AT&T policy of opposing regulation, Vail went even further; so long as it met his standards and specifications he welcomed it.

Three years later, in the 1910 AT&T annual report, he said the essence of correct regulation should be: ". . . such as to encourage the highest possible standard in plant, the utmost extension of facilities, the highest efficiency in service, and to that end should allow rates that will warrant the highest wages for the best service, some reward for high efficiency in administration, and such certainty of return on investment as will supply all the capital needed to meet the demands of the public."

But if this seemed radical to observers, it was minor compared to his 1915 San Francisco speech to the National Association of Railway Commissioners. In it he detailed his specific ideas on regulation.

Regulators should think of themselves, he said, as juries charged with "protecting the individual members of the public against corporate aggression or extortion . . ." Regulators should see it as their duty "to restrain and suppress . . . certain evils that have been ingrained in our commercial practices," and also "to restrain an indignant and excited public."

The head of a great corporation speaking of "corporate aggression or extortion" and "evil . . . ingrained in our commercial practices," would be unusual enough today, but was nothing less of astounding in 1915. It justified Thomas Edison's assessment made in 1912: "Until his day the telephone was in the hands of men of little business capacity. Mr. Vail is a big man."

Larger than Life

Brooks writes: As Vail approached old age he became more avuncular than ever—a rather portly man with a full white mustache and eyes that were both kindly and commanding. His many trips around the country to visit Bell System installations and see Bell System people were always the occasion for a series of parties. His private railway car, on arriving at a destination, would immediately be plugged in to local telephone and electric services, and after six o'clock the local telephone officials would be piped aboard—for whiskey and, of course, conversation about anything but business (his rule was "no business talk after six o'clock").

Theodore N. Vail

There is a too-good-to-be-true quality about Vail, and a skeptical observer finds himself searching for the man's mortal mistakes. What separated him from other leading industrialists of his time—that hard-shelled and rather narrow breed—was the openness of heart and broadness of mind that enabled him to see both sides of the great questions, and the courage, or aristocratic detachment, to state both sides openly.

Perhaps his special qualities as an industrial leader—his need for tranquil thought, his refusal to be hurried, his love of his work and pride in it—are most succinctly suggested in what he once said about himself and Harry Thayer, his closest professional associate (whom he always addressed simply as "Thayer") and eventually his successor as president. "Sometimes," Vail said, "old Thayer comes in to my office and we just sit and look at each other."

Passage

Theodore Vail died on April 16, 1920, at Johns Hopkins hospital in Baltimore. He was 74 years old. The Vail medal was established in 1921 to be awarded to employees "in recognition of unusual acts or services which conspicuously illustrate the high ideals which governed the policy of Mr. Vail as to public service."

The entire world owes Theodore Vail a debt of gratitude, not only for contributions realized in his day but for those which bore fruit years later, from seeds he had planted; this is, perhaps, the truest mark of greatness.

Mr. and Mrs. Gardiner G. Hubbard

4

Gardiner Hubbard, Father-in-Law of the Telephone

Without the efforts and influence of Gardiner Hubbard the world would in all probability never have heard of Alexander Graham Bell. Further, the Bell System would never have existed and the evolution of telecommunications would have been vastly different. The introduction of many of the technological marvels the world now enjoys—from lasers to cellular telephones—would have been delayed for many years. Gardiner Hubbard was the man whose vision, energy, and perseverance evolved the telephone from a crude novelty to its place among the most useful and profitable devices ever created. The events culminating in his arrival on the scene, however, constitute a series of coincidences so extreme as to risk being termed ludicrous if they should ever appear in a work of fiction.

Background and Beginnings

Gardiner Greene Hubbard was born in 1822 to a Massachusetts supreme court justice whose American ancestry dated to 1635. He graduated from Dartmouth in 1841, studied law for a year, then went to work in a leading Boston law firm.

Hubbard was an energetic and effective attorney who also possessed the conviction and energy of a born promoter. He organized the world's first street railway line outside of New York City, between Cambridge and Boston. He also established a water supply system for Cambridge and organized the Cambridge Gas Light Company. As a patent attorney he took a special interest in inventions promising faster and cheaper communications, particularly enhancements to telegraphy. This interest became the obsession which led to his role in the development of the telephone.

Mabel Hubbard; Bell's Wife to Be

It is seemingly unfair, but sometimes true, that misfortune in one avenue is required to open doors in another. Hubbard's daughter Mabel had become totally and permanently deaf as a result of scarlet fever when she was five years old; if she had not, it is likely Alexander Graham Bell would have labored in obscurity while others claimed fame and fortune from the telephone.

Hubbard, who was determined Mabel would have as normal a life as possible, had begun a relentless and far-reaching search for help in teaching her to speak. With very few exceptions the only vehicle for communication among the deaf at that time was sign language. Teachers capable of helping the deaf learn to read lips, let alone to speak, were almost impossible to find.

The tenacious Hubbard's confidence was not shaken by early difficulty in finding help for his daughter, however. True to his take-charge spirit he became a champion for the cause of teaching the deaf to communicate through speech. His inspired work with the Massachusetts legislature to improve education in this area became his personal mission. The stopper came when he brought eight-year-old Mabel before a Massachusetts legislative committee; she thoroughly impressed its members with her lip-reading skills and her ability to speak even though totally deaf. The committee soon after approved a $50,000 endowment for the Clarke Institution for Deaf Mutes, which was chartered in 1867 at Northampton, Massachusetts.

It was at the Northampton school, in 1872, that Hubbard first meet Bell. From this meeting, which took place only because of Mabel Hubbard's deafness, the stage was set for the next act in this remarkable drama.

Multiple Telegraphy Meets Its Match (Maker)

Hubbard had long been a crusader in search of a technology that would permit multiple telegraph messages to be sent over a single wire. This would make telegrams cheaper, he reasoned, and would make swifter communications available to more and more people. Further, he had a plan through which his proposed "United States Postal Telegraph Company," would partner with the U.S. Postal Service to send, pick up, and deliver inexpensive telegrams as part of normally scheduled mail deliveries. The public would benefit, and Hubbard the entrepreneur would earn a well-deserved fortune.

The obstacle to implementing his plan continued to be the lack of workable technology. There had been some advancements in this area, but the giant Western Union Company, which would have suffered greatly had Hubbard's scheme materialized, immediately bought all rights for their use. Hubbard was becoming discouraged when young Professor Bell, speech teacher of sixteen-year-old Mabel, came to visit the Hubbard house one Sunday afternoon in October 1874.

After tea Bell played the piano, which led him to demonstrate that a piano would echo the pitch of a note sung into it; this oddity was a basic example of the fundamental principle of multiple telegraphy Bell was then seeking to perfect.

Bell's demonstration and subsequent explanation led Hubbard to believe he had found his long-sought solution. A partnership was formed between Bell, Hubbard, and Thomas Sanders, whose deaf son George was also a pupil of Bell's. Per their agreement Hubbard and Sanders would provide financial assistance for Bell's multiple telegraphy experiments and the three would share equally in any returns. Bell had not only secured desperately needed financial support but had also obtained two experienced partners with his best interests at heart.

Patent Number 174,465

Work on multiple telegraphy gradually fizzled, giving way to its more advanced cousin, the speaking telephone. Here the story jumps ahead to the winter of 1875-1876; Bell and Watson had successfully made improvements to the telephone and the time for filing patents had arrived.

In order to secure both U.S. and European patents Bell had refrained from filing in the United States due to an agreement with a Canadian businessman and politician named George Brown. Per their agreement Brown would secure the foreign patent rights for Bell. He would also provide money for the privilege of participation in the venture. Their agreement was contingent on Bell delaying the U.S. filings so as not to jeopardize the foreign patents. As time dragged on and Bell had not received money or even communication from Brown (who was in Europe), Hubbard urged Bell to go ahead and file the U.S. patents.

Bell, whose sense of obligation was sometimes strong to a fault, refused to do so until he had heard from Brown. Bell and Hubbard argued but Bell would not be moved. On February 14, 1876, without Bell's knowledge, Hubbard took action and filed the patents himself on Bell's behalf. Later that very same day the Chicago inventor Elisha Gray filed his own patents for a speaking telephone. Thus, by a matter of a few hours and with thanks to Gardiner Hubbard, Bell owned first claim to what would become the most valuable patent ever granted.

The Right Connections

Hubbard's Cambridge connections were instrumental in rounding up both Harvard and M.I.T. scientists for Bell's first public lecture and demonstration of the telephone on May 2, 1876. This led to a much larger M.I.T. lecture three weeks later. These lectures and the resulting newspaper stories led to rapidly growing interest in the telephone. Admission to the lectures cost fifty cents per person, which generated the first money the nearly destitute Bell had earned from his invention. The first thing he bought was a commissioned silver replica of the telephone as a gift for Mabel, who later became his wife.

The Centennial Exhibition

On June 25, 1876, the telephone was given a tremendous boost through its demonstration for Emperor Dom Pedro of Argentina and for the British scientist Lord Kelvin. This took place at the United States Centennial Exhibition in Philadelphia. From this point on public knowledge of and demand for the telephone grew dramatically. Few people, however, are aware of the behind-the-scenes role Gardiner Hubbard played in making this historic occasion a reality.

First, Hubbard was one of three committee members for the Massachusetts education and science exhibit. In this capacity he made sure space was set aside for the display of Bell's telephone and multiple telegraph; this was critical since the deadline had already passed for entries in the electrical section before Bell thought his telephone ready for showing.

Second, although Dom Pedro had already accepted Bell's invitation to observe the telephone at the Exhibition, Hubbard telegraphed his future son-in-law to hurry to Philadelphia two days earlier than planned. He set him up in the same hotel as that of three judges in the electrical competition. Before the night was over Bell had met and talked at length with two of them about his exhibit. The stage was set for the smashingly successful demonstration before Lord Kelvin and Emperor Dom Pedro, which would remain among Bell's favorite reminiscences.

To Lease or Not to Lease

Along with increasing demand for telephones, a debate grew among Bell, Sanders, and Hubbard as to whether the instruments should be leased or sold outright. Money was very short, and the faster cash from outright sales would have greatly helped the immediate financial situation. Hubbard, whose views eventually prevailed, strongly favored leasing. He argued that if telephones were sold outright it would be very difficult to prevent unauthorized persons from illegally manufacturing them.

Hubbard's feelings also came from his having been an attorney for the McKay Shoe Machinery Company. This visionary company had reaped tremendous profits by charging royalties for shoes made on its patented machines. As it turned out, maintaining control of telephone manufacturing through leasing also allowed for efficient maintenance and repair. Further, it provided significant cost savings through economies of scale; this favored the formation of a universal network and the rise of a single dominant service provider in each geographic market.

The Hiring of Theodore Vail

As if Hubbard had not done enough, he added yet another feather to his cap in 1878 when he hired Theodore Vail as general manager of the fledgling Bell company. The specifics of those events have already been examined, but too much can never be said of the contribution Theodore Vail made to furthering the spirit of service in telecommunications. If not for Gardiner Hubbard, however, Theodore Vail would never have become part of the rich heritage of the Bell System.

The Company is Named

Alexander Graham Bell's place in history was already assured as the inventor of the telephone; the almost universal recognition of his name, however, must be credited to Hubbard's proposal to name the company after the inventor. This was good business strategy at a time of intense competition from all sides, but Hubbard more than once credited his concern for his son-in-law's permanent fame as his motive. Robert V. Bruce, in his biography of Bell, describes the genius of the name selection this way:

The four-two-one progression (Alexander Graham Bell) of syllables gives the name a gathering force and culminating impact. The last syllable itself has the initial blow, metallic peal, and liquid diminuendo of the age-old communications device it echoes. The name "Bell," moreover, goes well with the first syllable of "telephone." Its sense is fitting to the instrument...the name lends itself to a simple, shapely, instantly recognizable emblem, so that Bell's name survives as a device of corporate heraldry...

Passage

Gardiner Hubbard died on December 11, 1897, from complications due to diabetes. In his seventy-five years he left his mark in many areas and kept his vision squarely on service to others.

Charles Fleetford Sise on his voyage around the world.
Melbourne, Australia, 1868

5

Charles Fleetford Sise, and the Telephone in Canada

The early histories of the telephone in Canada and the United States are forever linked through the lives and work of two great men.

Alexander Graham Bell conceived the fundamental idea of the telephone in 1874 at Brantford, Ontario, while on an extended visit with his parents. The inventor loved Canada, and for 37 years made his home near the beautiful village of Baddeck, Nova Scotia.

Charles Fleetford Sise embodied the spirit of service in every aspect of his long and venerable life. From sea captain to soldier to businessman, he insisted on honest dealings and always gave at least as much as he got. He was widely respected and admired throughout his years at the top of the Canadian telephone business.

Family Heritage and Beginnings

The Sise family is traceable to the early 16th century and the English parish of St. Ives, in Cornwall, England. The branch of the family which would eventually produce the Senior Statesman of the Canadian telephone industry took root in Ireland, at Castle Lyons, in County Cork, Munster. Edward Sise, born there in 1762, would cross the Atlantic to North America in 1784.

His arrival in the New World in December of that year was memorable although he would just as soon have forgotten it; after running out of food while crossing the Atlantic, sixteen of the forty-two hungry people on board died when the ship was wrecked on Salters island just off the Massachusetts coast. Edward Sise was able to swim to shore with nothing but the clothes on his back, barefoot, soaking wet, and nearly freezing in the pitch black December night.

After his rescue from the island the next morning, Sise eventually moved to New Hampshire. It was there that he started the prosperous shipping business that would become a deeply ingrained part of the family tradition and heritage. The sixth child born to Edward and his wife (the former Ann Hodgdon) was Edward Fleetford Sise, who would become the father of Charles Fleetford Sise. Young Edward became a dealer in crockery, glassware, and coal, then added an insurance agency, all in Portsmouth, Massachusetts.

Charles Fleetford Sise was born there on September 27, 1834. "Charlie" to his friends, the boy early on felt the call of the sea, and made his first voyage at age sixteen on board the *Danube*. In 1856 he was made captain of the *Annie Sise* at the age of twenty-two, and then began a distinguished career in merchant trading.

Captain Sise

One particular story that demonstrates Captain Sise's decisiveness while in command occurred in England in 1858. The *Annie Sise*, loaded and ready to sail from Liverpool, was under instructions to wait for two passengers. But the barometer began to fall rapidly and Sise's instincts warned him to get out of the dangerous shallow waters; he ordered the anchor raised and sailed without the passengers.

For six weeks, after news of the devastation on the west coast of England reached the owners of the *Annie Sise*, they feared she had been sunk. When they received a message that she was instead safe in the destination port they were deeply grateful for Sise's good judgement and quick action. To show their appreciation they presented him a gold watch with the letters C-H-A-R-L-E-S-F-S-I-S-E marking the hours.

In his years of sailing the captain survived numerous other near calamities. From these experiences he developed the trait of making extremely fast decisions when called for, although he was superb in hearing and weighing all sides of an issue when time allowed. His ability to know what was urgent and what was not became a major factor in his later successes.

Sise in the South — the American Civil War

As a result of shipping in the Gulf of Mexico Sise decided to make the American South his home. He was married in February 1860 to Clara Bunker of Mobile, Alabama; later the couple moved to New Orleans. Along with many Americans Sise viewed almost with disbelief the gathering crisis of the Civil War. When war came Sise chose the side of his adopted South.

The only chapter in his military service about which any specifics are known was written between March 5 and June 10, 1862, when he served as a corporal in the Crescent Regiment of New Orleans, joining in the fierce fighting at Shiloh.

While few facts are known about his Civil War days, legends abound. Foremost among them is that he was the private secretary to Jefferson Davis, the president of the Confederacy. Many believed that Sise, as an intelligence officer for the South, carried out a number of brilliant missions. Years later, in Montreal in 1881, Jefferson Davis himself spoke of the wartime service Charles Fleetford Sise had rendered. "No one," he said, "would ever know how devoted the service had been."

A consensus of unsubstantiated opinion holds that Sise's main participation was as a blockade runner moving goods in and out of the besieged Southern ports. His involvement in that bloody war ended in 1863 when a plan to sell Confederate bonds in England, then return with supplies, fell apart after he reached Great Britain.

Whatever his role in the war, it will be forever shrouded in mystery and legend. Sise himself seemed to enjoy adding to the confusion, often ending a reminiscence abruptly by saying, "That is a closed chapter now. Let it stay closed. There is much in life that is best forgotten."

The Second Career

In 1867 Sise captained the Annie Sise in a 405 day voyage around the world, from New York around the Cape of Good Hope to Australia and back to New York. At that time, following the death of his father, he ended his seafaring life and joined the Royal Canadian Insurance Company.

In 1872 his wife Clara died, leaving behind three young daughters, although the youngest died that year, also. The next year Sise remarried, to Caroline Pettingwell, and together they had three sons over a period of six years.

Sise put himself energetically into his work and did very well, eventually achieving the post of resident manager of the Royal Canadian Insurance Company for the United States, residing in Boston. From the beginning, however, he found himself under personal attack for a variety of groundless allegations apparently stemming from resentment for his role in the Civil War; it was too soon after that war for a Northerner who had served the South to command the public confidence in a Northern city.

The Royal Canadian defended him publicly and privately, but on August 2, 1879, Sise formally notified the company of his resignation. In spite of the attacks on his character he had many supporters, as evidenced by this excerpt from the September 1879 issue of *Index*, an insurance industry publication:

The United States manager of the Royal Canadian, Mr. C.F. Sise, has acted with a regard for the interests of that company which made his own personal interests an affair of secondary importance. With a contract under which he could have held the company for some years to come, he has apparently simply asked himself, "What is the best thing, from a business standpoint, for the Royal Canadian?" Whatever others may say, we believe Mr. Sise has discharged his duties in an honorable and highly creditable manner.

Had anyone predicted in the late autumn of 1879 that the beleaguered Sise stood on the threshold of a third career, one that would write a notable chapter in industrial history, such a prophecy would have seemed improbable at best. The fact was that at the age of forty-five he was out of a job.

Sise Answers the Call

His affiliation with the Royal Canadian was soon to open other doors, however, in a totally new direction. In a letter dated January 17, 1880, to Andrew Robertson of the Royal Canadian, Sise presented his view of an upcoming meeting this way:

The Bell Telephone Company is making its arrangements for Canada and wishes to see me on Monday on the subject. The plan of the directors will probably be to give to good parties the whole field. It is, however, desired that these corporations be as much Canadian in their personnel as possible, and they want to secure the best people in Canada.

Sise had Canadian connections, which is exactly what the Bell company needed. His mission was later detailed in a letter from W.H. Forbes, President of the National Bell Telephone Company of Boston, including:

To organize a company to be called the Canadian Telephone Company, for the purpose of holding the Bell Telephone patents...throughout the Dominion of Canada. The Capital Stock (unless further advised) should be two hundred and fifty thousand dollars.

To harmonize the conflicting interests of the telephone business, getting if possible the Dominion and the Montreal Telegraph Companies to give up their respective telephone agencies, upon the condition that a consolidated telephone company shall be formed to work impartially between the two telegraph companies...to develop the telephone business.

Accompanying Forbes's letter was a memorandum drawn up by Theodore Vail, then general manager of National Bell, calling for the incorporation of two companies. The first, Company A, would be a holding and manufacturing company. It would own the telephone patent rights (most notably Canadian Patent No. 7789) and supply instruments for use in Canada. Company B would be the operating company; an application for its charter was already under consideration by the Canadian Parliament.

Negotiations Begin

Sise reached Montreal on March 9, 1880, and immediately set to work on his imposing task. Reporting to President Forbes on March 10 he confirmed what the National Bell company already believed, that the telephone situation in Canada was ripe for consolidation. The two chief companies, the Montreal Telegraph Company and the Dominion Telegraph Company of Toronto, operated their telephone lines chiefly as feeders for their telegraph business. Neither had found their telephone ventures to be profitable. Both, Sise believed, could be convinced to sell to an independent company provided neither benefitted at the other's expense.

He reported that the total telephones in use in Canada at that time, which he believed could be increased to over 5,000 within a year, were:

Town	Edison Phones	Bell Phones
Montreal	300	250
Toronto	50	200
Hamilton	50	300
Quebec	40	75
Ottawa	50	50
Other Towns	200	600
Totals	690	1,475

While Sise was correct in judging the Montreal Telegraph company ready to sell its telephone operations, the situation with Dominion was altogether different. He entered into an extremely sensitive period of negotiation which lasted for months and revolved around rival interests and conflicting personalities. Many times the proceedings seemed on the verge of collapse.

It was through these negotiations that Sise's genius for service through leadership and diplomacy became apparent. His years as master of the *Annie Sise* had accustomed him to being in command, to making decisions on the basis of his own judgements. Further, his experience with the Royal Canadian had taught him that in business more was often needed than a quick yes or no. He had learned the lesson well; there were few men who could be more adamant when firmness was needed, or could yield a point more graciously.

Planning Ahead

The negotiations also made it clear that Sise would be crucial to the new company after consolidation, as there was no question the shaky structure would crumble without him. It was critical to assure the Canadians whose services he had already enlisted that he would remain to direct the operation.

After discussion of the issue in a series of confidential letters between Forbes and Sise, Forbes offered a position at a salary lower than Sise had requested. Forbes said National Bell might be willing to increase the amount "...if Canada proves a more profitable field than we anticipate." He ended by saying, "I do not feel that it is absolutely necessary that you should make up your mind about this question at the moment. Why not complete the organizations, look the ground over, and then decide?"

In Sise's judgement, however, the time for a decision had come. He replied to Forbes's letter the very next day: "I am very glad you have treated the matter in the same frank manner in which I wrote you. In justice to the company, this should be settled now . . . I will come here and take the active

131

*Andrew Robertson, first president
of the Bell Telephone Company of Canada*

management of both companies. I trust—and believe—that the result will prove satisfactory to all concerned."

Sise became vice president and managing director of the operations company, with Andrew Robertson of the Royal Canadian as its first president. Theodore Vail would for the time act as president of the holding company, with Canadians rounding out the management of both.

The Deal is Concluded

Consolidation between the Montreal and Dominion Telegraph Companies finally occurred on November 1, 1880. As envisioned, Bell Telephone of Canada became strictly an operating company. The Canadian Telephone Company, Ltd., held all patent rights and supplied telephones to Bell

Telephone of Canada on a rental and royalty basis. This arrangement lasted until October 28, 1882, when Bell Telephone of Canada bought from the Canadian Telephone Company all patent rights with the exception of one—the Duquet Patent—which the Canadian Telephone Company retained solely as a reason for continued existence. Sise voiced his opinion to Forbes that such an arrangement would be pointless, but the Canadian Telephone Company continued in existence for twelve more years before it was finally disbanded.

Commitment and Integrity

Poised for rapid expansion, the first task confronted by management of the new company was organizing and streamlining basic operations. On the question of rates, which were not then regulated, Sise had definite ideas: the rates must yield a reasonable profit, yet they must be as low as circumstances would permit. Low rates were necessary to establish the foundation, the base, on which future profits could be produced. His policy on rates and service was concisely stated in a September 1887 letter to a complaining Montreal customer:

We do not claim our service is perfect. A new business, based on a discovery not ten years old, must meet with many difficulties which are only to be overcome with experience and expense. But I can say with truth that this company has never taken advantage of its practical monopoly, but has adopted every improvement as soon as it was known, and has endeavored to give the public the best service at the lowest rate compatible with the interests of its shareholders.

Despite his support of the South in the Civil War Sise's heart remained in the New England of his boyhood. He sorely missed Boston and reminisced often about old friends there. Yet, in November of 1881, when offered a tempting position in Boston, his commitment to duty was evident in a letter to a friend who had urged him to accept:

133

I have been thinking over the matter and, while I consider it one of the most desirable positions in Boston, I am of the opinion that I would not be acting fairly towards either the National Bell Telephone Company of Boston, the Bell Telephone Company of Canada, or the Canadian Telephone Company, Ltd.

The first sent me here to take care of their interests on my own terms; the Directors of the two Canadian Companies accepted those position solely out of goodwill to me—from our old relations in the Royal Canadian—and not one of them would remain for a day on the Board if I resign. You can understand that if I give up my position and the entire Boards of both Companies were to resign, the stock would go to pot, and the Companies would be seriously injured. I have never done an unfair thing knowingly—and don't want to in this case.

Contributions

In addition to managing the company past formidable obstacles during its birth and early growth Sise left his mark in a number of areas. These include:

Right of Ways

The right of way for telephone poles in streets and alleys was a priority in which Sise would not yield or compromise. He was well aware that telephone progress in England had been hampered by the absence of such rights. The telephone company there had regularly been forced to string its lines on the roofs of buildings, resulting in an unsatisfactory quality of service.

Although in its charter Bell of Canada had explicitly been given the right to "construct, erect, and maintain its lines. . . along the sides of and across or under any public highways, streets, bridges, water-courses, etc.," it was constantly defending itself from attacks and litigation. Examples include the newspaper editor who cut down the pole in front of his office with an axe, and a court case which Bell of Canada lost in which a horse, frightened by the barking of a dog, dragged the carriage it was pulling into a telephone pole.

In 1905, thanks to Sise's prodding, the Privy Council delivered a favorable and far-reaching judgement; the company's authority to use the streets and highways for its poles and conduits was clearly established from that point on.

Manufacturing

A matter nearly as critical as secure right of ways involved manufacturing. Under its original charter the company was empowered to manufacture, lease, and sell telephones and instruments for use in connection with a telephone or telegraph company. In 1882 the manufacturing privilege was extended to include "such other electrical instruments and plant as said company may deem advisable." This was critical in that the company's growth had outstripped the production capability of qualified vendors. It found it must produce its own supply or lower the quality of the service it was committed to provide.

In 1895 Sise launched the Northern Electric and Manufacturing Company, Limited. Four years later a plant for covering iron and copper wire was also acquired, which in 1911 became the Imperial Wire and Cable Company. These two companies were combined in 1914 as the Northern Electric Company, Limited, which later became industry leader Northern Telecom.

Fire Alarms

Sise knew from his experience in the insurance business that most of the fire-alarm systems in Canada were obsolete or inadequate. He was also convinced that the Bell Telephone Company was in the best position to introduce and maintain an updated system. In 1884 he arranged for the company to become the Canadian agent for the Gamewell Fire Alarm Telegraph Company. The first system was installed in Winnipeg and subsequently introduced in a number of towns and cities. The involvement of the Canadian telephone company greatly improved the responsiveness of local fire departments and thereby prevented the loss of untold lives and property.

An Early Divestiture

In the company's first annual report, covering operations for 1880, Sise and President Robertson noted that the company had been established by a special act of Parliament, "for the purpose of working the entire telephone system of Canada." Over time, however, Sise managed the transfer of the telephone systems to locally operated enterprises in many provinces. These included Prince Edward Island in 1885, the Maritime Provinces to the Nova Scotia and New Brunswick Telephone Companies in 1888, British Columbia in 1889, Manitoba in 1908, and Saskatchewan in 1909. Today each continues an excellent telephone system under autonomous local management.

Telephone Pioneers of America

Sise was among the first to sign up for membership in the Telephone Pioneers of America upon its founding in 1911. His legacy will endure through the Charles F. Sise Chapter of that organization, located in Montreal.

Passage

Charles Fleetford Sise died on April 9, 1918, after a three day illness brought on by pneumonia and accelerated by his then advanced age of eighty-four years. He had retired as president three years earlier but had remained active as chairman of the board until the time of his death. Nearly twenty years later William Patten wrote the following tribute to Mr. Sise:

The charge committed to him, he administered as a public trust. He held strongly that a great public service corporation should be a good public servant and this attitude was constantly impressed upon every official and employee. From the very inception of the business he insisted that service must come before economy, that no bargain was a good bargain unless it benefitted both parties.

Part Two

The Service Ethic Today

6

The Service Ethic in Telecommunications

"A robot can do a good job, but only a human being can enoble work with a great attitude, and by so doing touch it with the magic of humanness, make it come alive and sing, make it truly worthwile."

Earl Nightingale

"To love what you do and feel that it matters—how could anything be more fun?"

Katharine Graham

Getting the Right Perspective

There is an old story about two laborers breaking up rocks with sledgehammers. One was wearily lifting and half-heartedly swinging the big hammer, his face haggard and drawn. The other was swinging energetically, whistling all the while, his body and the sledgehammer moving in a crisp, tireless rythm.

"What are you doing?" the first man was asked. "I'm breaking these rocks up," he groaned, then with tremendous effort raised his heavy hammer to let it fall again. But the second man, in response to the same query, said in a loud and excited voice, "I'm helping build a cathedral by breaking these rocks up to be used in the construction! It's going to be beautiful, a thing of grace and majesty that will stand for a thousand years! Excuse me, but I need to get back to work!"

Accordingly, our perceptive determines how we see the value of our work, how we view its importance and its contribution to the world. W. E. B. Du Bois, a founder of the NAACP, put it beautifully when he said, "The return from your work must be the satisfaction which that work brings you and the world's need of that work. With this, life is heaven, or as near heaven as you can get. Without this—with work which you despise, which bores you, and which the world does not need—this life is hell."

Service and Telecommunications

Arguably, nowhere is the spirit of service more evident than in telecommunications. Dedication to serving the public has become deeply ingrained in telephone people, largely due to the telephone being so instrumental in summoning aid in times of emergency. This first occurred in January 1878, when 21 physicians were summoned to a railway disaster through the doctor and drugstore telephone network in Hartford, Connecticut. Since emergencies cannot be predicted in advance, service must be extremely reliable virtually all of the time. When service is interrupted no effort or expense is spared to restore it.

There is an old Bell System film in which the actor portraying a telephone lineman is preparing to go out into a raging storm. When a non-employee friend asks him why he doesn't wait for the storm to let up he explains it like this: "When the wires are down we put them back. And if you're not naturally that way, why, this business will make you that way."

Angus MacDonald and the Blizzard of 1888

The much-publicized "snow hurricane" of March 1993, which pummelled much of the eastern U.S. and Canada, invited comparisons to the great blizzard of March 1888. Back then, however, nearly all telephone lines were above ground and vulnerable, suspended above city streets on poles reaching ninety feet tall and crowded with as many as 300 wires. The potential for a major service disaster was huge.

The 1888 storm struck before dawn; by noon it had created the greatest disruption of daily life of the entire nineteenth century. Most telegraph lines in Connecticut were knocked out, and New York City lost all telegraph and train service. Minimal local telephone service was maintained without interruption in New York, however, as well as one long distance circuit each to Philadelphia, New Haven, Albany, and Boston.

By the following afternoon the telephone system of America's largest city was in shambles. The long restoration, which would not be complete until May, had already begun. Reconstruction costs were so great that the Bell company's earnings were reduced by half; two quarterly dividends were skipped altogether. The public, which had been clamoring with increasing volume against the eyesore of the overhead wires, now demanded action. A program to place the wires underground commenced almost immediately.

It was during the blizzard, along the New York-Boston-Maine route, that lineman Angus MacDonald became part of the rich tradition of telephone lore. MacDonald and the other members of his crew walked the toll route day and night through the howling storm to keep the vital communications link open. As if this wasn't enough, they also trudged through waist-deep snow with food for stranded passengers on a train cut off from the world by the drifting snow.

The Spirit of Service is a painting by artist Frank Merritt depicting MacDonald during the blizzard. It has come to symbolize the service ethic and dedication to duty of telephone workers everywhere. Although the original painting has been lost, a replica now hangs in the Association offices of the Telephone Pioneers of America, in Denver. After retiring from the Bell System Mr. MacDonald remained active in the Pioneers for many years. He died in 1958 at the age of ninety-four.

The World Trade Center Bombing

The dedication to service restoration during times of crisis remains as strong today as it was in 1888. Whether the cause of an outage is hurricanes, earthquakes, fires, riots, tornadoes, terrorism or floods, the spirit of service has prevailed again and again.

There are many heroic service restoration efforts that could have been cited here, but one of the most recent examples is the World Trade Center bombing. New York Telephone was commended by the New York Public Service Commission, the U.S. Congress, and the media for its handling of that disaster, which occured on February 26, 1993. The blast killed six persons, displaced 70,000 workers, and created a service nightmare. During the first four days of the crisis New York Telephone kept service working by, among other things, installing a combined total of 176 circuits in one-third of the time usually required. And this was just the beginning.

Rinker Buck, publisher of *Brandweek* magazine, was among those giving high marks for New York Telephone's efforts. "Following a contingency plan put in place for just such emergencies," Mr. Buck wrote in *Brandweek*, "New York Telephone's operations crews swung into action before the smoke had even cleared. Phone technicians were climbing the stairs to reach vital switching stations even as thousands of frightened employees were being evacuated. Within days, in this domestic equivalent of Operation Desert Storm, dozens of phone systems and computer links were restored in remote locations."

U.S. Rep. Jerrold Nadler (D-Mahattan) commended the company for keeping the lines of communication open on the day of the bombing, providing the only link to the outside world for terrified workers trapped in the towers. "The staff of New York Telephone planned effectively and worked swiftly to ensure that the network continued to function," Nadler said. "The people of New York City have reason to be grateful to the New York Telephone Company for so quickly and skillfully adapting to this crisis."

Brandweek also praised the ads which began to run almost immediately after the bombing, and through which New York Telephone communicated information and reassurance to displaced businesses and their employees. The ads told affected persons how to re-route their calls via call-forwarding technology to their homes or other locations. The ads had to be direct and informative, but could not in any way appear competitive or opportunistic. *Brandweek* said, "In an age of complexity, where natural and manmade disasters disrupt the basic technologies we have come to rely on, New York Telephone has shown the way."

Doug Mello, New York Telephone's group vice president-Manhattan Market Area, said simply, "Our goal was to deliver a well-coordinated and managed response, and our employees have executed that plan admirably."

The spirit of service: a telephone tradition that is here to stay.

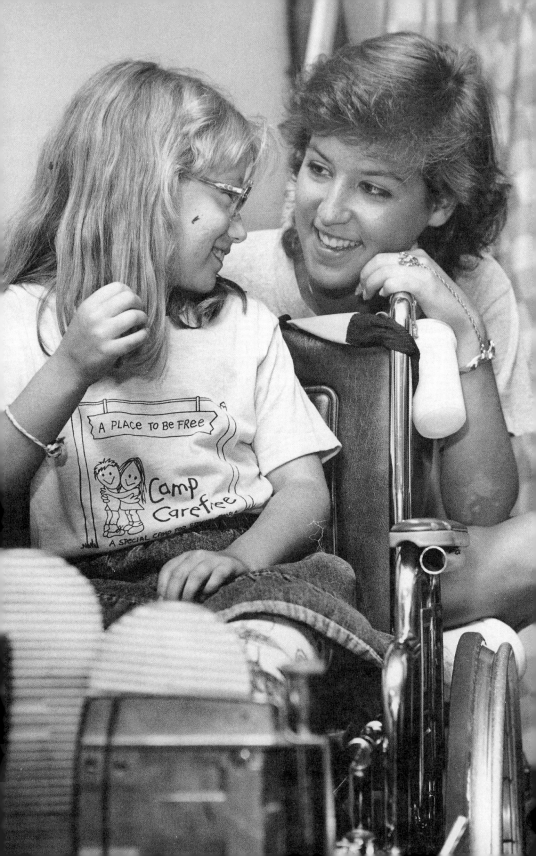

7

The Telephone Pioneers and the Way of Service

> "Do all the good you can,
> By all the means you can,
> In all the ways you can,
> In all the places you can,
> At all the times you can,
> To all the people you can,
> As long as ever you can."

> John Wesley

There is a place where the Bell System lives on, the *original* Bell System, the one that did business in both the U.S. and Canada when the speaking telephone was still a brand new gadget in a world that didn't quite know what to make of it. It is a magical place of kindness and commitment, a very human place of love, sweat and tears. It is the world of the Telephone Pioneers of America, a group that has probably provided more service to the less fortunate than any comparable organization in the world.

Today the Pioneers are over 800,000 strong, spreading their magic of community service and fellowship throughout the continental United States and Canada. But what is the essence of Pioneering? What is the secret of their success? Why has this organization continued to survive and flourish through the great depression, two world wars, and the break-up of the Bell System? How did it evolve from its original, social-oriented focus to become the largest and foremost industry-affiliated community service organization in the world? We'll explore the answers to these questions here, and take a brief look at the very large and open hearts of the modern day Pioneers.

I. Beginnings

The germ of an idea for the organization was conceived in 1910 when three veteran telephone employees—Henry Pope, Charles Truex, and Thomas Doolittle—wrote down the names of all the old-timers they could think of. All three were prominent telephone people who had been a part of the industry almost since its inception. Pope had organized the National Telephone Exchange Association and presided at its first convention at Niagara Falls in 1880. Truex had been active in the business since 1879, hired by Theodore Vail to establish exchanges throughout the U.S. Doolittle, an innovator, had made many contributions to the improvement of telephone service, the most notable being the invention of hard-drawn copper wire; its superior conduction abilities over that of the previously-used iron wire was a huge step toward making long distance transmission practical.

As the idea for an organization began to take shape, the three founders enlisted the support of Vail, who enthusiastically embraced the idea of (what was then) a social organization for veteran telephone employees. "We have all worked together to the same end and to the same purpose," Vail wrote, "and it is only fitting that we should sometimes play together."

With Pope as the driving force the three drafted a formal membership paper dated October 1, 1910, which they distributed to all the early telephone people they could reach. Word spread, and within a year there were 493 members. Alexander Graham Bell was granted the honor of being named the first honorary Pioneer.

The first meeting was held in Boston on November 2 and 3, 1911, with 244 Pioneers (nearly half the total membership) in attendance. Theodore Vail was elected president, and would be re-elected president every year until his death.

Issues were discussed and voted on by the attendees, and several speakers talked of the early days of telephony. But the highlight of the day, the reason many of those present had come, was to hear a speech by the inventor of the telephone.

"I feel it a little presumptuous upon my part to try to speak of the telephone to telephone people," Alexander Graham Bell began. "You have all gone so far beyond me. Why, the little telephone system that I look back upon—what is it compared to the mighty system that goes through the whole extent of our countries today? It is to you that this great development is due, and I feel that it behooves me to speak very modestly of the little beginning that led to this great end. I belong to the past, you belong to the present."

The Road to Service

While service has become synonymous with the Pioneers, this was not always the case. Volunteerism evolved as an off-shoot of the Pioneers' hobbies programs, designed to help members make the transition from full-time jobs to retirement. The seeds of volunteerism were also nurtured by the dedication to service deeply ingrained in telephone people by their obligation to fulfill a public trust.

It was at the 1958 Pioneer General Assembly, held at the Statler-Hilton hotel in Chicago, that community service, long a focus of Pioneer activities, was officially declared a part of their mission. The theme of that meeting, Community Service, was illustrated by a banner showing the Pioneer triangle flanked by six crests symbolizing areas of participation— civic, health, education, youth, welfare, and church. Pioneer president William Kahler, also president of Illinois Bell Telephone Company, called service to the community "The New Tradition" and made it the major point of his address.

The early Pioneers passed on to us a great tradition, an unchanging obligation to do our part, be it little or large, in maintaining the ideals of our industry and our country. Part of that obligation requires that we create some traditions of our own . . . you have

149

demonstrated your willingness to take up that challenge.

In the Telephone Pioneers of America, we have literally an army of men and women who are organized into Chapters, Councils, and Clubs, in thousands of communities throughout the United States and Canada. Here is a force whose long-established tradition of telephone service is about to be crystallized into an effective pattern for community service.

We have a great history and a great heritage. We have here made a good start in building a new tradition, our own tradition if you will. Now we need only remember that to do something worthwhile requires us to do more than pass a resolution. It requires work, and the Telephone Pioneers of America are uniquely capable of that.

Thirty years later, at the 1988 Dallas General Assembly, the Pioneer symbol was modified with the addition of the now famous words under the triangle: "Answering the Call of Those in Need." The Pioneers continue to answer that call with the result that the world is literally a better place.

A Sampling of Service Projects

Mr. Don Fleischauer of Petoskey, Michigan, a member of the Pioneers' Great Lakes Chapter, sent the following summary of newspaper headlines bearing testimony to the widespread contributions of the Pioneers. "At one time the Telephone Pioneers were the best kept secret," Mr. Fleischauer wrote. "Today, newspapers throughout the United States and Canada carry articles on the generosities of the Pioneers."

New York Herald:	"Telephone Pioneers have Major Involvement in Olympic Torch Run"
Minnesota Gazette:	"Telephone Pioneer Fundraising Buys Two Wheelchairs"
Chicago Tribune:	"Telephone Pioneers Focused Efforts on a Home for Children Separated from their Families"

Atlanta Record Eagle:	"Telephone Pioneers Wage War on Alcohol and Drug Abusers"
Toronto News:	"Telephone Pioneers Raise $3,000,000 for Restoration of the Statue of Liberty"
Vancouver Echo:	"Telephone Pioneers Sponsor Aid to Immigrant Youth"
Waterloo Courier:	"Telephone Pioneers Donate Handmade, Specially Designed Tricycles to Handicapped Children"
Albany Sunday Herald:	"Telephone Pioneers donate Time and Materials When Installing Lifelines"
Oregon Bulletin:	"Telephone Pioneers Donate Hearing Aid Dog"
Arizona Sun-News:	"Telephone Pioneers Donate Therapeutic Devices to Rehab Center"
Reading Times:	"Telephone Pioneers Donate Braille Writers to the Blind"
Spokane Republic-Extra:	"Telephone Pioneers Plant Flowers and Trees along Highway"
Houston Post:	"Telephone Pioneers Adopt Angels through Salvation Army"
Kansas Independent Reporter:	"Telephone Pioneers Build and Donate Safe Playground Equipment to Accommodate Handicapped Children"
Wisconsin Reporter:	"Telephone Pioneers Build Ramp at Fishing Access to Accommodate Wheelchairs"

Michigan Gross Pointe News:	"Telephone Pioneers Sponsor Screening Program to Catch Infant Hearing Loss Early"
Columbus Enterprise:	"Telephone Pioneers Donate Time and Materials to Build Bridge in Historical Park"
Muncie Evening Post:	"Telephone Pioneers Donate Crocheted Slippers and Lap Robes to North End Nursing Home"
Albany Sunday Herald:	"Telephone Pioneers Sponsor Teen Dance"
Winston-Salem Journal:	"Telephone Pioneers Give Party for Patients at Hospital"
Florida Forum:	"Telephone Pioneers Make and Donate Audio (Beeper) Balls to Blind"
Cumberland Times:	"Telephone Pioneers Stage Variety Show, Proceeds to Convalescent Home"
Reading Times:	"Telephone Pioneers Donate Stove and Refrigerator to Needy Family"
Morristown Daily Record:	"Telephone Pioneers Donate Telecommunications Devices (TDD) to the Deaf"
Nashville Banner:	"Telephone Pioneers Make Beeping Eggs and Sponsor Easter Egg Hunt for Blind Children"

Get Involved—It's Proven Good for You!

In their book, *You Can't Afford the Luxury of a Negative Thought,* authors John-Roger and Peter McWilliams describe the benefits of service to the server as well as to those being served:

Service, as we define it here, is the art of taking such good care of yourself that you cannot help but take good care of others. When you fill yourself with love, happiness, and compassion, the desire to share the overflow of these with others is automatic.

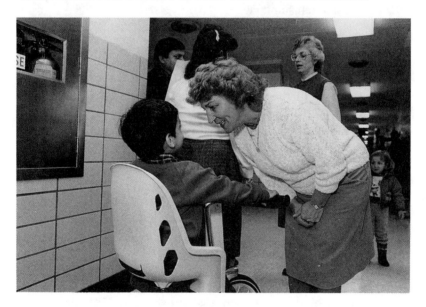

It's one of the great open secrets of the world that by serving others you serve yourself. As Emerson said, "It is one of the beautiful compensations of this life that no one can sincerely try to help another without helping himself." Those who have given to others for the joy of giving know that the reward is just that—joy.

Besides feeling good and knowing that you have done good for others, an article in the May 1988 issue of *American Health* claims that doing good for others is physiologically good for you. A study in Tecumseh, Michigan, for example, showed that doing regular volunteer work—more than any other factor—dramatically increased life expectancy. The article concluded, "Those who did no volunteer work were two and a half times as likely to die during the study as those who volunteered at least once a week." The article also explained that doing good for others enhanced the immune system, lowered cholesterol levels, strengthened the heart, decreased chest pains and generally reduced stress.

One interesting study at Harvard showed that even thinking about doing service produced positive physiological results. Service can be done in any number of ways. Even from bed. The phone is a marvelous tool of service with which you can—to quote Ma Bell—reach out and touch someone.

Calling all Volunteers!

Research indicates only about ten to fifteen percent of Pioneers actively participate in local projects on a regular basis. Many of those who have not participated say they have never been asked to do so. If you have been meaning to get involved but haven't yet made the time, please consider this a personal invitation on behalf of your local Pioneer Chapter. Pick up the phone and call your Chapter office, or simply ask the first employee or retiree you meet with a huge smile on his or her face—the odds are good that smile got there as a result of involvement in a Pioneer activity!

II. Hurricane Andrew

The strength and responsiveness of the Pioneers were dramatically illustrated in August 1992, when hurricane Andrew slammed into Louisiana and south Florida. Response from Pioneers around the U.S. and Canada was nearly instantaneous, beginning even before the disaster areas had officially asked for help. Patricia Rainey, a Pioneer from Delray Beach, Florida, said that when the storm ended, ". . . I immediately sent a check to my Pioneer chapter for I knew in my heart all the money would be used in the best way possible to help the victims. That sums up my total belief in Pioneering."

Patricia Rainey was not alone. Two weeks after Andrew's visit Florida had received over $125,000 in Pioneer donations, and Louisiana over $28,000. The logistics involved with receiving, sorting, storing, and distributing the steady stream of incoming deliveries were imposing, but the Pioneers took things in stride. Working twelve to fifteen hours or more per day they made sure food was sent to the hungry, medical supplies to the sick and injured, clothing and household goods to those who had lost everything, and of course Hug-a-Bears to help dry the tears of the frightened children.

Have you wondered what happened to all those Pioneer Hug-a-Bears sent to the hurricane-damaged areas? The following letter is from Mr. Vic Yannotti of the Pioneers' Sunset Life Member Club based in Plantation, Florida. Mr. Yannotti provides a first person account of how the bears were distributed, and what it was like to be of service to those in the disaster area in the aftermath of the storm. He asked we share it with our readers, and we are pleased to do so. We hope it reinforces your decision to provide assistance if you did so, and that it will make you even more willing to participate the next time your help is needed.

"Many of the boxes of Hug-a-Bears we received had letters or notes requesting information on how the bears were used," Mr. Yannotti wrote. "It would be impossible to respond to every Club and individual so I thought I would write up some of the ways in which the bears were used and share some of Rita's (my wife who is also a Pioneer) and my experiences while distributing them. Believe me, every one of the 7000+ bears we received was used and appreciated! Our heartfelt thanks go out to every Chapter, Council, Life Member Club, and every individual who participated in this effort. It was a major accomplishment and made me feel very proud to be a Pioneer!"

Andrew and the Bears
by Vic Yannotti

It all started with a call for help from the Telephone Pioneers Gold Coast Chapter office—water was needed, canned food, flashlights, coolers, etc., also Hug-a-Bears for Andrew's victims. Since we live in an area which was only slightly affected by the storm we alerted our neighbors and collected all their hurricane supplies along with clothing and blankets.

I was then the acting Teddy Bear Chairman in Dave Smith's absence—he had asked me to take over while he went on extended vacation, telling me, "Don't worry, Vic, it's always slow during the summer." I donated all the Chapter bears we had in stock (96) along with twenty-five the Sunset Life Member Club had available. I immediately called all the Life Member Club presidents who were not on vacation and urged them to donate all the bears they could, to be distributed to the hurricane victims' children. Shortly after, we received a call from the Broward Sheriff's Department that bears were needed for their cars that were patrolling the devastated areas. Forty-six bears arrived from one of the Life Member Clubs and we immediately donated them to the Sheriff's Department. Margate, another city we normally supply, called for bears;

156

they were assisting the Homestead police and had used up their supply. We gave them 45 bears that had just arrived and were now completely out except for eight bears we saved for

emergencies (as if this whole thing wasn't emergency enough)!

Dan Ahearn, the Life Member Manager for South Florida, had acquired a grill and needed volunteers to cook for the first Saturday after the storm in Perrine, which was one of the hardest hit areas. Rita and I and about a dozen other volunteers cooked 1500 hamburgers, 1500 hot dogs, plus beans and chili and provided iced tea and other soft drinks. The people were thankful; for some this was their first hot meal since the storm. I gave my last eight bears away to children in the area. These children had lost everything and their faces really glowed when they saw the bears. I wished the eight had been eight hundred.

The bears continued to trickle in during the week and were sent to the distribution center for immediate availability to the south Florida area, except for a few I put aside in case we received additional calls from the sheriff or police department.

The next week I was told a tractor trailer load of bears had arrived at the warehouse. I immediately called Patti DeBrown, Chapter Administrator, and asked if we could make arrangements to put bears on the desks of all the children in

the lower elementary grades on the first day of school, which was the following Monday. She agreed, and Dan Ahearn contacted the Board of Education to find out which schools were affected and how many bears would be required. But before the Board could get back to us we found out that the bears belonged to the Red Cross, not the Pioneers, and that we could not use them! When we heard back from the Board we still told them we could handle their four worst affected schools; we had only a few hundred bears when we made that commitment, not nearly enough!

We put out a call for help and bears soon started arriving in a steady stream from Pioneer Chapters all over the country as well as Canada. We went to work unpacking the bears and re-packing them in groups of 50 for delivery. When workers in the warehouse would run across Hug-a-Bears on an incoming truck (the trucks were loaded with all manner of food, clothing, tools, etc.) they would rush them back to us. By 2 p.m. that day we had 1300 bears, enough for our first three schools. We told our fourth school we would deliver on Saturday even though we did not have a single bear left after we packed the van. We were counting on the Chapters to pull us through.

We got to the schools with difficulty. There were no street signs or traffic lights, as they had been flattened by the storm, and all the police officers were from somewhere else. I asked an officer for directions and he said he only knew the number of the street he was on, and told us to ask the officer on the next corner. That person turned out to be a National Guard member who could provide no help whatsoever. But somehow we found the first school and got directions to the other schools from there.

All the schools were damaged. One had a leaking roof and we walked through several inches of standing water to deliver the bears. The Armed Forces had cleaned the debris out of the school and taken up the wet carpets. The second school was dry but had no air conditioning. The principals of the two schools had lost their homes but were determined the schools would open and save the children from being bussed several hours each way to Miami or north Dade County. All the teachers and principals were overjoyed to see us and the bears (maybe it was the other way around). These people were working hard to get their schools running as close to normal as possible even thought the majority of them had lost their own homes and belongings. They had even managed to have the children's names on their desks for the first day of school. Our hearts went out to them.

We returned to the warehouse that evening and found our confidence in the Chapters was rewarded; more bears had arrived! We returned the following morning and found still more had made their way to us! We needed 450 and by 12:30 p.m. we had our bears thanks to our friends from around the country.

A total of 1700 was delivered to South Miami and placed on the children's desks. Our efforts and those of all Pioneers who made and contributed bears were rewarded by the feedback we received. The children held the bears and would not let them go. We heard from principals and teachers alike that the bears were clutched tightly even during nap time.

On Sunday, September 20, we were watching the news and saw a piece on a school that was opening the next day, one week late. It was heavily damaged and the Navy Seabees had worked long hours to get it ready. Many of the teachers had also worked long hard hours even though they also had houses damaged and destroyed. I called the TV station to get the location of the school, which turned out to be in the Cutler Ridge area of Miami which was heavily damaged. I arrived at the warehouse at 5:30 a.m. and collected nearly 500 bears and took off for Cutler Ridge. There were still no street signs or traffic lights, and traffic was horrendous.

Off the main streets traffic was limited to one lane because of debris piled on both sides of the road. These were upper-middle class homes that were destroyed and the possessions and personal items which had been purchased with so much thought and feeling lay strewn along the sides of the road as so much garbage—bicycles, mattresses, sofas, TVs, boats, mangled cars, broken trees, stuffed toys and all sorts of odd shaped pieces of houses and insulation everywhere. The debris was being picked up by huge trucks which hauled it away to burning sites which, by then, were marring the skyline with black smoke spirals. The trucks inadvertently dropped pieces of the debris as they made their way to the burning sites and there was always the danger of tire punctures. One of the teachers I talked with had three flats within a week.

After many false starts I arrived at the school (two and one half hours to go approximately 40 miles). When I explained why I had come the teachers were elated. I was escorted to all the pre-kindergarten, kindergarten, first grade

plus a handicapped children's class and passed out the teddy bears. We went to the library where the old stuffed toys were all wet and mildewed and left twenty bears with them. Each teacher I visited also received a Hug-a-Bear (they deserved it!). The children were overjoyed and their first class project was having a picnic lunch the next day with their new bears. It was worth the effort to see not only the faces of the children but the joy expressed by the teachers and principals as well. A TV crew was at the school and interviewed me and I told the children and the TV interviewer that these bears were made with love just for them by the Telephone Pioneers, and had come from all over the country. Unfortunately, the interview was never shown on TV.

On September 25 we again loaded up a van with 750 Hug-a-Bears and visited five tent cities' first aid and medical units to pass out bears for their young patients. We also gave bears to two day care centers and a tent that was used for counseling both children and adults. The bears were well received at all locations. Nurses treating young patients were especially happy to receive them and, in many cases, they directed us to other medical units. The bears were also great for gaining access to the tent cities which were allowing only official vehicles. When a stern-faced M.P. approached the van and asked what we wanted, a teddy bear would change that face to a smile and we would be granted access immediately.

On September 30 we delivered 2500 bears to the Dade County Board of Education at their request, to be used by counselors of children in the worst affected areas. On October 2 we loaded a truck with the 500 remaining bears and a large amount of school supplies and children's clothes. The clothes and school supplies went to the Florida City school, which is in a hard hit area and serves some of the migrant labor camps. The bears were delivered to four remaining first aid stations and, as in all past occasions, were well received. This was our final group of bears.

Rita and I wish to extend thanks to all the participants in this endeavor for allowing us to bring a little sunshine to the lives of these children who had gone through so much and are still enduring a very traumatic experience. By all counts we distributed over 7,000 of your bears, and many more passed through the warehouse and out to the hurricane areas without our involvement.

Our special thanks also to the people at the warehouse for their cooperation. Even though everyone was working at 110 percent or more they still had time to find those Hug-a-Bears when a new truck came in. Our thanks particularly to Pat Caruso, Moni Garceau, Brenda Jones, Doc Wheeler, Ron Czaplicki, and Walt Pace for all their help, and to Bill and Joanne Wingender for those fine lunches (which in many cases turned out to be breakfast, lunch, and dinner).

We were both happy to have worked with the warehouse gang and were even sort of sad to see it end, but very glad from the standpoint that the facility was no longer needed. And I have one suggestion for Dave Smith—the next time you decide to take an extended vacation during the summer, please advise the National Hurricane Center so they can be prepared for the unexpected!

III. Pride in Pioneering Essay Contest

How does it feel to be a participating member of the Telephone Pioneers of America? What are the rewards of fellowship in the cause of service to others? Since valid answers to these questions can only come from persons who have experienced the joys of Pioneering first-hand, we asked them! Following are selected excerpts from entries in the "Why I'm Proud to be a Pioneer" essay contest, followed by the top three entries in their entirety.

"...Consider a few of the many things that make Pioneering so appealing. You can be in direct contact with those you help; you can see first-hand the results of your work. You have the freedom to choose from a large variety of activities that are available. You can spend as much time helping others as you desire, particularly the retirees who have more free time now that they are no longer working. An important motivator is the built-in reward system that gives one a great feeling of satisfaction, knowing that you have contributed to someone else's welfare."

> Thomas F. Doyle
> Prairie Village, KS
> Gleed Chapter

"...I am so proud to be a Pioneer. To see the faces of joy and hope on the many people I encounter as I go about my volunteer activities. To know what I do is making a positive difference in a person's life. To be able to give something back to our sponsoring companies. Just to be able to say I am a Pioneer!"

> Evelyn Gist
> Los Angeles, CA
> Los Amigos Chapter

"...What unites us? Is it the history of dedication that stretches back to the Pioneers' founding in 1911? Is it the ideals summed up in our motto, 'Answering the Call of Those in Need?' Is it the goals we hold dear: Fellowship, Loyalty, and Service? Is it being in the same occupation? Yes to all these and more! Pioneering has personally helped me to develop my potential as a volunteer and as a person."

> Ted Berg
> Chicago, IL
> Theodore Vail Chapter

"...Pioneering has managed to survive divestiture and from the ashes has emerged a whole new breed of Pioneers. They're younger, energetic, and constantly finding new ways to serve their fellow man. There's no way to tell how many lives have been touched because Pioneers cared enough to get involved."

> Doris W. Knight
> Valdosta, GA
> Dixie Chapter

"...I'm proud to be a Pioneer and feel passionate about it, because I believe the organization exemplifies the best of the free enterprise system...As a Pioneer I have been closely involved with several schools; since I have a background in Computer Science I saw how underutilized computers are. I don't think computers are the answer to all our problems, but I do believe proper utilization of distance learning, interactive multimedia, graphics, virtual reality, and eventually holographic images merged with computers can give us a quantum leap, and could put us back in the lead. As our CEO Ray Smith put it, 'Since we are heavily involved in bringing in the dawn of the information age that makes us the information brokers.' I sincerely believe we as an industry have an obligation to take the initiative to accelerate the effective use of telecommunications and computers in the 'classroom without walls' of the future."

> Ken Oexmann
> Manalapan, NJ
> H.G. McCully-Upstate Chapter

"...I'm proud to be a Pioneer for it has made me humble and grateful; it could have been me that someone else was coming to rescue...I have found joy in serving."

> Alma Wallace Byrd
> Spartanburg, SC
> South Carolina Chapter

"...Pioneers can move mountains. It is a special group of caring people. One of the best ways to meet with old friends and make new ones. Never a dull moment. Everyone can help in their own way. Everyone is welcome. Rewards are numerous. Join today!"

Linda Merrill
Huntsville Life Member Council
Alabama Chapter

"...I have learned through Pioneering that giving of yourself to benefit others is a blessing. To receive the riches of a child's smile and to see the happiness of a senior citizen that comes from just knowing someone out there cares about them..."

Darlene Johnson
City of Commerce, CA
Los Amigos Chapter

"...I am so proud to be a part of New Jersey Bell, my sponsoring company, for supporting me as a Pioneer. In the many things we undertake we work hard to make the company proud of our commitment to the community on its behalf."

Alberta Willis
Roselle, NJ
H.G. McCully-Upstate Chapter

"...My favorite part of 'clowning around' as part of our chapter's Smilemakers Clown Troupe is visiting with seniors. What a wonderful bunch of people! What a greeting you receive when two or three clowns walk into a hospital room! Doesn't everyone love a clown? You can see it in their faces! Visiting the children's ward can be sad. I guess one can understand elderly people being in the hospital, but it's a lot tougher when one sees sick kids—and they love to see a clown! The only problem the Smilemakers have is not enough hours in the day. People are always phoning and asking if the Smilemakers are available to help them out. But as much as we want to help we can't possibly do all that is asked of us. Most of us work and also have families and other activities as well. I'm sure we could use at least twice as many clowns in our troupe and still need more!"

> Elaine Baron (Pioneer Partner)
> Regina, Sask.
> Saskatchewan Chapter

" . . . In my forty-and-a-half years on the job I enjoyed every day of it and would go back to work again if it was permissible, as I was treated royally. There have been a lot of changes since I retired 25 years ago, but I am happy with my pension and good benefits at my age of ninety."

> Margaret Cote
> Laconia, NH
> Vermont-New Hampshire Chapter

"...Quoting Mr. Dave Miller, president of the Oklahoma Chapter, 'Employees retire. Pioneers don't.' This more or less sums up why I'm proud to be a Pioneer and always will be."

> Maria Menchaca
> Eagle Pass, TX
> Life Member James E. Olson Chapter

"...My husband started with the company as a splicer in November 1962. He loved the job and took it seriously. Many nights he'd come home tired and cold. There were also many evenings he would be called back out, especially after storms,

166

but he never complained. I was proud of this man because he did his job from his heart. Sad to say, thirty years later George passed away. Now, whenever I see a telephone truck I quietly say a little prayer to that big brawny Pioneer of mine. This is why I had to change the title of this essay to "Why I'm Proud to be a Pioneer's Wife."

> Mrs. George Reilly
> Bloomfield, New Jersey

"...I think back to March 1992. I remember following the Rodney King trial on television every day. I remember exactly where I was when the verdict in the case was read. I remember driving through the city of Compton, California, feeling as if I was moving in slow motion through some war-torn third world country thousands of miles away. I remember the fear I felt and the silent prayers I prayed that evening, when most felt the need to blame, the need to destroy, the need to point that accusing finger. It was then that I knew something had to be done. Not just politically, but with loving kindness. Something to show the communities that there is someone who cares, someone who can help. It was two months later that I started my first year as a Telephone Pioneer."

> Willett Skinner
> Los Angeles, CA
> Los Amigos Chapter

"...When I am 73 instead of 37, I expect my life will be different. I imagine my walk will be slowed, my vision will be dimmed, perhaps my enthusiasms will be cooled. But I expect my pride in Pioneering will still be strong."

> Becky Woodworth
> Bellaire, TX
> San Jacinto Chapter

"...I am eighty years old and am not a Pioneer. I am writing this in behalf of a very dear friend, Robert L. Tussing, who I feel should be recognized for what he has done as a Pioneer. He retired from the telephone company in 1977, moved to Florida with his wife and has not stopped working and helping people. He went to Central Florida Community College where he took up music and piano, but failed piano. He did not give up. He studied theology, was ordained in 1984, received a church, preached and taught retired people in Municipal Center on Wednesday nights. He is now working with retarded children. He also holds services at the Marion House, which is a Health Care Center for elderly people in wheelchairs. To me a Pioneer is a person who is willing to give his or her time and talent to help others without pay and be happy in doing it. This is such a person."

> Mary Meyers
> Ocala, Florida

"...The relationship we telephone people have is very special. In many cases we feel closer to our Telephone Pioneer friends than to our blood kin!"

> Mary Pearson
> Weatherford, TX
> Lone Star Chapter

"...Pioneers are part of a big family that shares not only projects but continued fellowship and friendship from year to year. My partner and I have made more friends than one person could ever hope for ..."

> Sequita O'Neal
> Milburn, OK
> Oklahoma Chapter

"...Pioneering helps me feel worthy and needed as I did while working for the company. It is an opportunity to see and socialize with my former fellow employees. Having worked for the company for thirty years I got to know a lot of telephone people. After nearly seventeen years of retirement it is a real joy to keep in touch."

> Tahlma Outlaw
> Riverside, CA
> De Anza Chapter

"...Although we know we cannot solve all of the complex problems in our communities we are able to assist those in need of our help and hopefully impact their lives in a positive way. In all of our projects, be it work with the homeless, building playgrounds or parks for the handicapped, assisting at hospitals or nursing homes, food banks or even cleaning parks and streets, the reasons for our success are simple - Pioneers helping people - unselfish donations of gifts and services as they spread their special rays of sunshine for all the world to see!"

> Leta Dixon
> Phoenix, AZ
> Coronado Chapter

"...We have been told we have the hearts of a martyr, the persuasive powers of a preacher, the strength of a rock, and the inventiveness of Alexander Graham Bell."

> Fay McIntyre
> Garden City, NY
> Paumanok Chapter

"...I can honestly say one of the greatest impressions in my life had to be my first quarterly meeting of the Telephone Pioneers.

It seemed almost unreal for me to believe this very large group of people came together to help anyone and everyone that needed it, with no expectation of pay. They received the greatest payment in the smile on a child's face or the outstretched hand of an elderly person..."

> Faye Kelley
> Columbia, TN
> Tennessee Chapter

"...It is my pleasure and pride to be a part of Telephone Pioneering. It reaches out in many directions and touches many people. It works both small and large 'near miracles.' It is caring, helping, doing and giving. It is willing hands and hearts of many volunteers with numerous talents and abilities performing services where there is a need. Teamwork makes many projects successful. That Pioneer Touch can be found from coast to coast!"

> Dorothy Rhodes
> Kansas City, MO
> Gleed Chapter

"...This wooden walkway in the Lord Sterling nature preserve, designed and constructed by the New Jersey Bell Telephone Pioneers, was built to enhance the sensory perceptions of the disadvantaged, those who experience the difficulties of visual, auditory, or physical handicaps. The path speaks vivid testimony to the spirit of those who genuinely care for their fellow human beings..."

> Timothy G. Murphy
> Jersey City, N.J.
> H.G. McCully-Upstate Chapter

I'm proud to be a Pioneer because of how it makes the recipients feel when we serve them and fulfill their needs. The first Pioneer function I participated in was a Christmas party for children with Spina Bifida. The person who asked me to go to the party requested that I dress up as a clown and entertain the children. The first problem was that I had no idea how to put on clown makeup and the second problem was I had no idea what I would do once I got there.

The morning of the party this person had me sitting at her kitchen table putting on the clown makeup. Another friend had made me a clown outfit. Once I was made up I said, "What do I do now?" The response was, "Don't worry, it will come to you."

When I walked in that room and saw the faces of those children light up I felt that my heart would burst. These children had problems that, only by the grace of God, I have never had to experience. Some children were walking with the aid of braces and walkers, some were in wheelchairs, and some had heads that were twice the size of their little bodies. I took a deep breath, entered the room and began to talk and play with the children.

When I left that party I went home and tried to sort out my feelings. I first felt sorry for those children but then I began to realize they didn't feel sorry for themselves. These children were happy. Even though they had what I considered to be insurmountable problems, they were happy and their love for me came shining through. From that day on I determined that Pioneering was for me.

I have been a Telephone Pioneer for many years and there always seems to be something new that we can provide for the community, the environment, and for each other. This organization doesn't care about your race, color, or creed, they only care about what needs to be done to improve mental and physical health for everyone and to improve the environment for future generations.

As president of the Century Chapter in Atlanta I have learned a valuable lesson. With the dedication of time and energy the Telephone Pioneers—including future members,

171

regular members, life members (retired persons), and partners —can move mountains.

I am proud to be an employee of a company that allows me to serve as an ambassador of goodwill. The best way I know to describe what Pioneering means to me is to say, "Pioneering is the Wind beneath my Wings."

Dorothy Fulcher
Atlanta, GA
Century Chapter

I first heard of the Telephone Pioneers of America when I attended one of my first meetings as a new employee of "Ma Bell." Over the next few years I continued to hear the word "Pioneer" in conversations with my fellow employees. However, it was not until I had accumulated enough service to be eligible to join that I gave serious thought to what it might mean to me to be a Pioneer.

I did know that, as a company and as employees, we pledged ourselves to raise business ideals. I also knew that as employees we come from every walk of life, we represent many different interests of the community, we are people of different religious faiths and different political persuasions, we are both "union" and "management" banded together in agreement that service to our customers and to humanity is the highest duty of mankind.

Perhaps most important, I had observed that the Pioneers were unified in their efforts to elevate and maintain a high standard in the social, political, business, and religious ideals of my community. And so, I joined at the earliest opportunity. Immediately, Pioneering provided a wondrous fellowship! I began to look forward to our meetings with anticipation and delight. Soon I realized that Pioneers are engaged in a great work—the work of making the world a better place in which to live, a better place in which to rear our children, and a better place for our senior citizens to share their golden years. A work in which our ultimate aim is not material return, but the deep satisfaction of the human spirit which we call happiness. A happiness which comes when we serve those who cry out for better conditions, better understanding, and greater opportunities for all.

There is often a tendency to promulgate high-sounding platitudes, and in the actual conduct of affairs to grow careless of them—not so with the Pioneers. There is no great gulf between that which they would do and that which they actually accomplish. They are masters at recognizing unmet needs in our communities: drug and alcohol abuse; the hearing, visually, mentally, physically, and the speech handicapped; recycling; crime. These are only a few of the community service areas in which Pioneers are active. Anywhere you find the sick, the lonely, or the disadvantaged, you will find the Pioneers.

Over the years I have particularly enjoyed working with children in many of our programs. In doing so I am constantly reminded of what Hildegarde Haethorne said about working with and teaching children: "Sometimes, looking deep into the eyes of a child, you are conscious of meeting a glance full of wisdom. The child has known nothing but love and beauty. All this piled-up world knowledge you have acquired is unguessed at by him. And yet you meet this wonderful look that tells you in a moment more than all the years of experience have seemed to teach."

How do Pioneers do it? Ask your Pioneer leadership, because those people work regularly to enhance your community's resources and to provide volunteer skills that are vitally needed. Whether it's community service, protecting our environment, or providing educational opportunities to the public, Pioneers are there.

Pioneers often take the lead in building those important bridges between related volunteer organizations and countless public, civic, and private agencies and organizations. Through my work as a Pioneer I have found many opportunities to become better acquainted with the leadership in my community and the chance to help make changes that improve the lives of others. Pioneers also learn that the work they do is motivated not only by personal satisfaction but also by tangible challenges and opportunities to improve individual skills.

"Pioneer"...a seven-letter word that means many things to many people but most of all means self-satisfaction. Pioneering opens the door to new ideas, new interests, and new problems you may never have known existed. It means the opportunity to see your club, your community, your state, and your country in an entirely new light. A great part of that self-satisfaction comes when you discover the family feeling that is the heart of Pioneering. A family feeling where pain is lessened by sharing with others and where joy and accomplishment are heightened when others are involved. The fellowship in your Pioneer Club, your Council, your Chapter, and among the Regions in the United States and Canada is a treasure to be shared.

Why am I proud to be a Pioneer, you ask. Perhaps William James said it best when he said, "The best use of life is to invest it in something which outlasts life." Pioneering offers many paths on which a Pioneer can move from problems to solutions, from dreams to reality as we strive for the blessings of peace—the peace to build and grow, to live in harmony and sympathy with others, and to plan for the future of our children and grandchildren with confidence.

Mary Beaver
Huntsville, AL
Alabama Chapter

Each one of us will come to a place in our lives when we will look back and evaluate our time on this good earth. For the reader to fully understand why I'm proud to be a Pioneer, I'll need to take you on a worded journey through my life, then you'll know why being a Pioneer holds the meaning it does for me.

As a young boy, I had an abusive mother and an alcoholic father. This life-threatening combination resulted in my sisters and my baby brother and I being taken from our parents and placed in foster homes. I have one particularly vivid recollection of an incident that happened just prior to our removal; my father spend most of his money on alcohol so there was never much left over to feed his family. I sometimes feel as if I spent the first seven years of my life being hungry. I had developed quite a skill—sneaking into the back of the Sunbeam Bread Truck as it made deliveries and helping myself to as much food as I could carry away. Then one day the driver caught me. Rather than chastising me he sent me on my way with the food I had stolen. I knew it was wrong to steal, but that man recognized the desperate hunger of a small child. His act of compassion has stayed with me all these years.

I refer to my years in foster care as my O.P.P. years (other people's parents). I had a chip on my shoulder because I wanted to live with my dad, and he was always promising me he'd get me back. He never did, and I lived with false hope for many years. Eight years and fifteen foster homes later I finally ended up with the folks I still know today as my parents—and they are Telephone Pioneers.

As a young soldier, I volunteered for duty in Vietnam. That year was the most physically and emotionally draining of my life, yet one that gave me a deep appreciation of what soldiers sacrifice for their love of country. Those young men of my generation served America at a time when our nation was divided over whether we should have been at war at all. After giving 100 percent of themselves to their country, these soldiers returned home to a country that wasn't willing to give them the respect they had truly earned.

There are so many volunteer organizations out there competing for membership, and we are attracted to these groups for different reasons. My foster parents, who I feel are responsible for turning my life around, were both Pioneers, so their early influence on my life has always been felt. When I found out about the Telephone Pioneers' long-term commitment to veterans and needy children, I was convinced that this was an organization I wanted to belong to, and it was a way to give back to the community, and make my little corner of the earth a better place to live.

The turning point for me is what I refer to as "My

Pioneer Moment." It's that moment in time when you realize that being a Pioneer really is something special. Let me tell you about my Pioneer moment.

This past year my Chapter learned about a 10-year old girl named Katie who suffers from juvenile-onset diabetes, a disease that dramatically restricts this little girl from leading a normal life. The Pioneers of my Chapter took care of a lot of Katie's medical expenses that weren't covered by insurance and that her parents couldn't afford; they purchased a One-Touch machine, a device that makes it much easier and more accurate for Katie to check her blood sugar level as often as needed. But the Pioneers went further than her medical needs, they bought Katie something she had always wanted but was out of her folks' financial reach. The Pioneers got Katie a pink mountain bike, and presented it to her at a fundraising dance in her honor. If you could have seen the smile on Katie's face that night, you would have been moved to tears. Katie lives in my small town, and every time I see her riding her pink bike I think of the love and compassion and generosity of the Pioneers, and the lifetime memory they made for Katie.

From the 7-year-old boy who stole bread from the back of a bakery truck, to the soldier who fought in the rice paddies of Vietnam, life can be a struggle to survive. But the Pioneers, and the people we help on our journey in life, make the trip worthwhile.

> Dudley H. Farquhar
> North Andover, MA
> Merrimack Valley Chapter

IV. The Future of Pioneering

In interviews with dozens of Pioneers from around the U.S. and Canada two consistent patterns emerged regarding the organization. The first was enthusiasm and pride in the fellowship and service Pioneering provides; the second was a desire for Pioneering to remain strong.

The Pioneers have received generous financial and moral support from their sponsor companies, beginning with Theodore Vail and continuing to the modern day telecommunications giants. Voluntary in every sense of the word, Pioneering is a tremendous asset for those sponsors, paying incremental dividends in employee morale, community service, and positive public relations. It is the sort of goodwill that can-

not be purchased by writing a check because it requires both the donation of the Pioneers' time and the opening of their hearts. Let us hope Pioneering endures as long as this big blue planet keeps spinning.

Part Three

Service
After
Divestiture

8

The End of an Era, the Start of a New One

"The breakup of America's telephone system, acknowledged to be the most efficient in the world, will affect nearly every aspect of our society. How all this came to pass is a frightening example of what can happen to a company recognized as one of our major national assets. It is a company that grew by its own efforts and with its own resources to become the world's largest business, whose Bell Laboratories led us into the information age."

Walter Annenberg, 1983

Do you remember when you first heard the U.S. government and AT&T had reached an agreement that would break the Bell System up into eight separate pieces on January 1, 1984? If you were an employee or retiree of AT&T or one of the Operating Companies—or employed anywhere in the industry, for that matter—the news probably came as one of the biggest shocks of your life.

Divestiture. The unthinkable and nearly incomprehensible. The news hit like a sledgehammer in the hearts and souls of the 1,000,000 or so men and women of that most noble of "natural monopolies," a term you don't hear so much anymore. Disbelief or denial was the reaction of many, followed by uncertainty and confusion as to what it all really meant. As "1-1-84" drew nearer, perhaps the most commonly shared feeling had evolved to one of loss. Of sadness. Of being forcibly separated from dear old Ma Bell, the grand old lady who had served so well.

And then the historic date came and passed and it was done. There was nothing to do but say good-bye. Good-bye to those who were assigned to AT&T from those in the Baby Bells, and vice versa. Yellow tape on the floors separated assets allocated to the new AT&T from those belonging to the local companies. New questions arose: Could we be partners? Could we still be friends? What were the rules? What in the world was happening here?

For a while things rocked along fairly well. There was a lot of bravado, especially among younger employees, about how the competitive world would now see the unleashed brains and muscle of the world's greatest company. But of course it wasn't the world's greatest company anymore. It wasn't even *a* company anymore; it was eight companies, one short of a baseball team, except now the players were on different teams.

For some employees the foreboding feelings took the shape of harsh reality in the early post-divestiture period. Downsizing, whether by early retirement, lay-off, or attrition became the new way of things. Friends left, some very excited at the prospect of starting a new career or retirement in their prime; others left in turmoil and tears, not knowing for the first time in their lives how they would pay their bills.

An Era of Transition

Whether we like it or not, life is change. The break-up of the Bell System was simply another chapter in a saga that is still unfolding. The transition has not been without hurdles or stumbling blocks, nor has service rated an A+ in every instance. Problems are a part of change, especially change of this magnitude, and are to be expected in spite of the best planning or intentions.

The constant factor, however, during this time of upheaval and renewal, the characteristic that has symbolized this industry from its beginnings, remains the spirit of service among its people. On the eve of divestiture, then-AT&T president Charles Brown summed this up when he outlined the requirements for future success in remarks made to the Telephone Pioneers of America:

> What has made the Bell System great has been its people at every level: operators, technicians, representatives, salesmen, saleswomen, secretaries, engineers, supervisors, managers of all types. The companies that succeed the Bell System will have these people to keep its greatness alive. A corporate reorganization, even the largest such reorganization in history, really cannot diminish the personal qualities which have long distinguished these people: integrity, dedication, enthusiasm, devotion to excellence. If we continue to display these qualities and to set an example for newcomers to our companies then we will surely live up to the trust placed in us by our predecessors, and the Bell System's heritage truly will become an enduring heritage.

The Decade Since Divestiture

How well have the divested companies lived up to Mr. Brown's prophecy? Have they indeed fulfilled the trust placed in them by their predecessors? A partial answer is found in the following chapters, which present year-by-year highlights from the annual reports of AT&T and the Bell Holding Companies (BHCs) from divestiture to the present. Please keep in mind that annual reports are written primarily for current and potential stockholders and therefore tend to emphasize the positive side of strategic initiatives, major milestones, and financial results.

These summaries also offer a valuable, time-lapse overview of many of the key events currently shaping the telecommunications industry. While the BHCs may have been born with a common parent and similar characteristics, each passing year has seen greater and greater differences in strategy, philosophy, and bottom-line results. Some of the companies have struggled to develop and execute strategies that complement their strengths; others seem to have known exactly where they wanted to go and how to get there . . . and have done so.

When all is said and done, however, only one thing is certain: there are emerging and evolving uncertainties on all fronts, including greater competition among the divested companies, that will make the second decade of divestiture at least as volatile and as interesting as the first.

9

AT&T

On August 24, 1982, the Consent Decree was approved by Federal District Court Judge Harold H. Greene. This decree called for AT&T to assign all responsibilities for local exchange service, long distance access service, Yellow Pages and cellular mobile communications to the newly created Bell Holding Companies (BHCs). As AT&T prepared for its new corporate mission chairman Charles Brown stated, "The company's overarching goal will be customer satisfaction."

1984

The first year of divestiture saw a greatly slimmed down AT&T emerge. As the BHCs were established AT&T went from assets of $149 billion to $35 billion. A company with a one hundred year history was suddenly a new company. In the process AT&T went from being comfortable "Ma Bell" in 1983 to a new competitive enterprise in 1984.

The new competitive environment caught AT&T facing rapid change and greater risk. At divestiture AT&T forecasted that it would earn nearly two billion dollars in 1984. By the end of the year the company had only earned approximately three quarters as much or $1.4 billion. Facing stiff competition and lower than expected financial results the company closed four of its manufacturing plants and froze management salary structures.

However, it certainly was not the case that AT&T had nothing to celebrate in 1984. Revenues for the year topped $33 billion as the company saw return on equity at nearly 9.5 percent. Nearly half of the company's revenues came from the sale of services, about a third came from product sales, and the remainder from rental revenues.

On January 1, 1984, AT&T Technologies was formed to assume the corporate charter of its manufacturing arm, Western Electric Company. AT&T Information Systems, formerly American Bell, was established to market business systems, enhanced services and consumer products on a deregulated basis.

AT&T Communications, formerly the Long Lines department, provides long distance services throughout the United States and to most of the rest of the world. At divestiture AT&T was the only long distance company whose prices and service offerings were fully regulated. Seeking the freedom to compete with other long distance carriers on even terms was and continues to be one of the company's key challenges.

One of the most significant events in 1984 was the entry of AT&T into the general purpose computer business. Many of the computer industry's basic inventions had originated at Bell Laboratories and AT&T had been making computers for its own use for many years. Computer hardware and software systems promised to play a major part in the company's strategy to provide integrated communications-based office automation systems.

Chairman Brown said at the end of 1984, "Difficulties will persist, of course, but what is now evident is the emergence of an altogether new enterprise eager to demonstrate its newfound market focus. Most of all, we expect to meet what is our most overriding goal: that is, to satisfy our customers, one by one."

1985

For the year, AT&T saw operating revenues up by 5.2 percent to nearly $35 billion. The effectiveness of cost controlling measures was reflected by the slower rate of expense growth of only 3.3 percent. The combined effect saw net income for the year up by over 13 percent to nearly $1.6 billion compared to the previous year's $1.4 billion. However, the company announced that while this was progress it still did not meet expectations.

Two main competitive challenges confronted AT&T. The long distance business continued to be a healthy and profitable contributor to the company; however, helped by massive subsidies decreed by the government, competitors continued to make inroads into the business.

While keeping an eye on their current bottom line AT&T also focused on the future. Expenditures on the order of $2.2 billion were incurred for research and development in 1985. The scope of these expenses covered activities such as basic research, new product design and development, and the enhancement of existing products.

Research activities included the exploration of optical computers that use light rather than electricity, the development of new mathematical formulas that allow for the quick solution of complex mathematical problems, and expanding the potential of fiber optics through technological modifications that allowed test networks to transmit the contents of a 300-volume encyclopedia in one second.

AT&T also responded to the needs of the local exchange companies—BHCs and non-BHCs alike—through the rapid deployment of digital switching. During the year 5ESS™ systems capable of switching 6.5 million lines were shipped by Western Electric. This was more than double the volume in 1984 and represented the largest, fastest and most successful product build-up in AT&T's history.

One of the goals stated by AT&T was to become the leading international provider of information movement and management products and services in the 1990s. By the end of 1985 the company had strategically placed 24 such offices around the world and was selling products in over 90 countries. Sales activities ranged from UNIX™ systems in Europe to the 5ESS switches in Egypt, Saudi Arabia and China, and also computers in Japan.

1986

In September of the year Charles L. (Charlie) Brown retired as chairman and CEO of AT&T. Elected to replace Mr. Brown was James E. Olson who had been serving as the president of AT&T.

As the year progressed AT&T had to confront a severe dilemma. There was no question in the minds of its top management that the company's business—information movement and management—held the promise of strong growth and global markets. However, the company was seeing flat earnings, high costs and mixed operating results in various parts of the business.

The clear sign from this self-evaluation was that AT&T needed to severely reduce the cost of doing business to a more competitive level. The company took steps to consolidate production, warehouse and other facilities at a cost of over $1 billion. Another $1.1 billion was charged against earnings as inventory was written down and depreciation charges were increased.

Despite these measures management decided that another action had to be taken. AT&T was forced to confront the fact that if it was to become more competitive it must become more efficient. Efficiency translated into a need to reduce the existing workforce—management and non-management alike—by approximately 32,000 employees, or 10 percent of its workforce. Another $1.1 billion was set aside to account for the cost of this workforce reduction.

While AT&T was squarely confronting its problems it was also enjoying some successes. One of the largest was in its clearly winning the balloting for equal access presubscription across the nation. More than three-fourths of all customers were selecting AT&T to be their long distance carrier. Over 66.5 million business and residence lines selected AT&T to provide their long distance service in 1986.

Building for the future while providing new services for current customers led the company to spend over $3.6 billion for capital improvements—primarily on the long distance network—in 1986. By the end of the year AT&T had expanded its high quality lightguide fiber routes to over 10,000 miles.

Companies as diverse as American Express, Burger King, Black & Decker, American Airlines and the U.S. government continued to rely on AT&T. The company's ability to quickly deliver information from around the world, while maintaining high levels of quality and service, spoke volumes of its commitment to the future.

1987

In 1987, AT&T finally achieved the key financial goal it had set in 1984. Revenues in 1987 were about the same as in 1984 and below those of 1986 and 1985 at $33.5 billion. Still, the company's net income eclipsed the elusive $2 billion level for the first time since divestiture.

AT&T had taken a series of painful measures in the post-divestiture world to reduce its cost structure. However, adherence to the corporate philosophy regarding quality and customer service was beginning to pay off.

An effort known as Project Turnaround was successfully launched. AT&T knew consumers were weary of the over-the-counter free-for-all in the telephone equipment marketplace. Cheap products had flooded retail outlets and frustrated consumers. Aggressive marketing efforts stressing product quality and customer service resulted in higher levels of market share and profitability for AT&T in the telephone equipment market.

During the typical business day customers made over 75 million calls worldwide on the AT&T network. International calling remained the fastest growing segment of this market with 2.6 million calls being completed daily. Responding to the battle for market share, AT&T's prices for long distance service came down over 15 percent during the year.

While voice calls still accounted for the largest amount of traffic on the network, digital services had become the fastest growing segment. With demand for digital services growing at 15 to 20 percent per year the company had converted 98 percent of its switching facilities to digital systems. Additionally, by the end of 1987 over 45,000 miles of fiber optic cable were in place.

The day-to-day operations at AT&T reflected the company's emphasis on quality and the efficiency of internal operations. Productivity growth in manufacturing operations averaged 10 percent during the year, about double the productivity growth rate for durable goods manufactured in the United States.

Progress was also made through the use of Just-In-Time (JIT) manufacturing initiatives. For example, at AT&T's plant in Shreveport, Louisiana, office communications systems that once took over three weeks to produce were rolling through the JIT assembly line in less than three hours.

1988

In April of 1988, after serving as the chairman of AT&T for less than two years, James E. Olson suddenly and tragically died. Named to replace him was Robert E. Allen who had been serving as the president and chief operating officer of AT&T.

From its ongoing operations AT&T was well positioned to enjoy record financial accomplishments. On revenues of over $35.2 billion, up from $33.8 billion the previous year, it would have been possible for the company to record net income of $2.3 billion, up 15 percent for the year.

However, the company decided to accelerate the digitization of its long distance network in order to better serve its customers. As a result, older analog plant and equipment was no longer of any value. A charge of $6.7 billion was absorbed to account for speeding up this modernization. Over $6.2 billion of this charge applied to the writedown of network analog equipment and associated support assets along with the removal of the equipment. The additional funds were for the costs of force reductions associated with this modernization.

In 1988 AT&T scored a major sales victory in the intensely competitive telecommunications industry when the federal government awarded 60 percent of the contract to replace the Federal Telecommunications System to a team led by AT&T. Over the next decade this contract could be worth up to $15 billion in revenue to AT&T.

The company also continued to make strategic investments. In January, an agreement was reached to purchase 20 percent of Sun Microsystems, a computer company. In July, a digital switching system joint venture with GTE was announced. And, at the end of the year, AT&T announced plans to acquire Paradyne Corporation, a data communications company.

The ability to transform research into revenue was proven when the KORBX® System was launched by AT&T's Advanced Decision Support Systems unit. KORBX grew out of a concept developed by a Bell Laboratories mathematician, Narendra Karmarkar, to solve complex network loading problems. As other companies saw how this system could help them solve their problems a revenue opportunity arose. For example, KORBX enabled Delta Airlines to plan highly efficient pilot flying schedules.

1989

Revenues and net income both achieved record postdivestiture highs in 1989. Revenues were up nearly $1 billion over 1988 while net income stood at $2.7 billion, an increase of $700 million. Assets climbed more than $2.5 billion to $37.7 billion as AT&T continued to invest and expand.

Nature shook the AT&T network on both coasts of the United States in 1989. The San Francisco earthquake and Hurricane Hugo teamed up to test the network's response to communications emergencies. Despite the turbulence in the communications marketplace over the previous few years AT&T was able to serve the needs of the nation during these emergencies as it had throughout its proud heritage.

In March, an AT&T division merged with the newly acquired Paradyne Corporation to form an operating unit called AT&T Paradyne. The objective of the merger was to produce the industry's broadest and most extensive line of data communications products. These products, such as the 6800 Network Management System, allow for the accurate and efficient movement of data around the world on ordinary telephone circuits.

AT&T's fledgling computer business began to gather strength during 1989. Commercial contracts were won with American Airlines, Firestone, United Parcel Service and Knight-Rider. An eight year contract signed with the U.S. Department of Transportation could eventually see the installation of up to 40,000 computer workstations.

Responding to competitive threats in the long distance business led AT&T to cut its long distance prices twice in 1989 and again on January 1, 1990. Over the previous five years the company had reduced interstate direct-dialed prices by nearly 40 percent. Still, long distance services accounted for well over one-half of the company's revenues.

At AT&T, serving the community also means giving financial and volunteer support for education, for the arts and for individuals in need. With a focus on science and engineering AT&T supported education with cash grants of nearly $15 million, computer donations worth $40 million and the loan of Bell Labs experts as visiting professors.

Besides continuing its support to the Telephone Pioneers of America, as the BHCs also continued to do, AT&T made grants such as $3 million to support the development of low-cost housing in New York and Chicago. The employees of AT&T also maintained a spirit of giving as could be seen from the $30 million they contributed to the United Way during the year.

1990

While showing a small improvement over the previous year, weaknesses in the U.S. economy slowed the growth of AT&T in 1990. Making a significant contribution to this slight upturn was the performance of AT&T's international sales. Revenues rose to $37.3 billion, up 3.1 percent from 1989, while net income climbed to $2.735 billion, up 1.4 percent.

For the first time since divestiture the AT&T Board of Directors authorized the company to increase its stock dividend. A 10 percent increase raised the annual dividend to $1.32 a share from the $1.20 it had been paying. With over one billion shares of AT&T stock on the open market this amounted to an additional annual payout of over $130 million to stockholders.

Positioning itself for the future, AT&T made its boldest move since divestiture. On December 6, 1990, AT&T initiated a cash offer of $90 per share, or $6.1 billion total, to fully acquire NCR corporation. NCR had developed a strong international presence in providing computer systems to the banking and retail industries. AT&T felt this acquisition would give it the critical mass needed to become a global competitor in the computing industry.

Another key move was management's decision to capitalize on AT&T's experience with telephone calling cards and enter the credit card business. Consumer demand for the AT&T Universal Card with its initial no-fee charter membership and 10 percent discount on AT&T long distance calls was such that by the end of the year it was the sixth ranked bank credit card in the United States.

Despite the weak economy, long distance calling volumes grew by more than 7.5 percent over 1989's record levels. By offering a variety of calling programs, such as the popular Reach Out® America plan, the individual telecommunications wants and needs of consumers worldwide were being met.

Building the network for future international opportunities saw new cable routes completed across the Pacific and the Caribbean in 1990. A project to lay new cable across the Atlantic was begun, and plans were announced to lay new routes to Australia, New Zealand and the People's Republic of China. The company made plans to have in place a transoceanic, optically amplified cable with the ability to simultaneously carry 600,000 calls by 1996.

1991

To fully appreciate the scope of the acquisition of NCR one needed only to review the revenue impact of that action. In 1990 AT&T recorded revenues of $37.3 billion while in 1991 that figure climbed to $63.1 billion, an increase of $25.8 billion, or nearly 70 percent.

The final purchase price of NCR was $7.5 billion and was consummated by exchanging 203 million shares of AT&T stock for full ownership of NCR by AT&T. Organizationally, AT&T's existing computer operations were merged into NCR such that the latter retained as much of its own identity as possible.

The focus of the "new" NCR was to be in transaction-intensive industries where computing and communications are highly interrelated. Banking and retail operations were targeted as among the areas where this interrelationship held great potential.

With the merger came the need to restructure AT&T so as to ensure future success. Charges of $4.5 billion were recorded as computer products and systems were consolidated under NCR, distribution systems were changed and the costs of underperforming investments such as real estate were disposed of.

Long distance service reliability remained the hallmark of AT&T's operations. The busiest calling day of 1991 was, as usual, the Monday after the Thanksgiving weekend. On that day the AT&T network handled nearly 158 million calls, and all but 211 of them went through on the first try.

Helping countries secure their economic futures also helped AT&T Network Systems International post nearly $1 billion in sales during the year. Providing digital switching in Poland, network management in Belgium, 5ESS switching in Taiwan and cellular equipment in the Dominican Republic were just a few of the international activities at AT&T.

At AT&T's equipment leasing arm, AT&T Capital Corporation, an additional 100,000 accounts were opened; this added $1 billion in assets to its portfolio. The AT&T Universal

Card continued its tremendous growth with over 12 million new cards being issued.

With its own line of cellular phones already in the marketplace AT&T announced its intention to expand the use of high radio frequencies, which it already held the license to operate. AT&T expressed its objective to widen its involvement in portable communications and to become a leader in wireless and personal communications services.

1992

AT&T had a banner year in 1992, recording record earnings of $2.86 a share on revenues of almost $65 billion. Wall street rewarded this performance by AT&T's stock trading at post-divestiture highs. It closed the year at $51 per share, up over 30 percent.

The crown jewel of the company remained the AT&T Worldwide Intelligent Network. From the United States a caller could direct dial more than 215 countries—with operator assistance another 65 could be reached. Circuit miles contained in the network could circle the world 80,000 times if laid end-to-end. The intelligent network may be thought of as a mammoth computer continuously being improved. For the year expenditures to maintain and improve this network reached $3 billion.

Early in 1992, the airline industry declared a fare war. A resulting avalanche of calls from travelers tested the network's capabilities. Record one-day call volumes in excess of 177 million calls were successfully handled. During an 11 day period over 1.6 billion calls were processed.

The 1991 merger of NCR's open systems approach to computing and AT&T's networking expertise continued to develop new products for consumers. A new NCR automated teller machine (ATM) application uses an AT&T Smart Card to verify a cardholder's voice print before permitting access to the customer's account. Smart Cards look like bank cards but have microprocessors and memory chips laminated within their plastic shells.

In the fourth quarter of the year AT&T stunned the industry by announcing negotiations with McCaw Cellular to form a strategic alliance involving marketing and technological cooperation. The company will invest nearly $4 billion in acquiring one-third ownership of McCaw, a clear signal of AT&T's intent to become a leader in the ongoing wireless communications revolution.

In 1993 with the tenth anniversary of divestiture only a few months away, AT&T's chairman Robert E. Allen said, "As we approach the new millennium, the power of technology is indeed bringing people together. By making those technologies easy to use, we can bring more capabilities to more and more people. This promises grand opportunities for human progress in all its dimensions."

10

Ameritech

Ameritech has its roots in the heritage of the midwestern Bell companies. The name Ameritech is the acronym formed from the company's original name: American Information Technologies. The base of Ameritech's operations is found in the operating telephone companies of Illinois Bell, Indiana Bell, Michigan Bell, Ohio Bell and Wisconsin Bell.

1984

In 1984, the Ameritech family of companies performed exceptionally well in the first year of the new era of communications. Ameritech delivered strong earnings with net income of almost $1 billion on sales in excess of $8.3 billion.

The company aggressively moved to provide new products and services, to seek new revenue opportunities, and to introduce new technologies to meet customer needs and fulfill their expectations well into the future. During 1984 over $1.7 billion was invested by Ameritech to maintain and modernize its network.

As a result of the modernization effort over 70 percent of the company's 14 million lines were served by electronic systems in 1984. Electronic switching expanded the market for profitable Custom Calling services such as Call Forwarding and Call Waiting. While total residence line growth increased only slightly in 1984, the number of customers subscribing to Custom Calling services increased over 15 percent.

During the year, the five Bell companies of Ameritech spent over $538 million on advanced communication technology. In 1984, Ameritech companies installed 19 digital switching systems and by year end the company had over 35,000 miles of fiber optic lines in service.

Along with divestiture came the opportunity to enter new competitive lines of business. Ameritech Mobile Communications was the first company in the nation to introduce commercial cellular mobile telephone service. This occurred in Chicago late in 1983. During 1984 cellular service was introduced in Milwaukee, Detroit and Cincinnati, serving 17,000 customers by the end of the year.

Ameritech Publishing was formed to assure continued leadership in the directory advertising market. In this increasingly competitive market the company achieved impressive results. Over 400 directories were published with a total circulation of 26 million copies, generating over $400 million in revenues.

As the first year for Ameritech came to an end the company was well positioned for the future. Mr. William L. Weiss, Ameritech's chairman and CEO, summed things up when he said, "We did everything we said we would do in 1984, and more."

1985

Ameritech made excellent progress on all fronts in 1985. Financial and operational performance were strong and contributed to the strength of the company's foundation for the future. The value of a share of stock in Ameritech, factoring in dividend growth and price appreciation, grew by over 45 percent during the year. Revenue for the year was up a little over 8 percent while net income was up almost 9 percent.

The key drivers behind the growth during the year included a strong increase in customer use of the network (for instance, intraLATA calling was up 12 percent); an increase of 124,000 business lines; and revenues from the new subsidiaries grew 34 percent to almost $700 million.

Toward the end of the year the company announced plans for its first major acquisition, Applied Data Research,

Inc. This company was one of the nation's foremost developers of systems software products, primarily for IBM mainframe computers. Applied Data Research was to provide the linkage customers were seeking between communications and computer systems.

To further enhance the marketability of Ameritech's advanced digital network services for business, all the services were brought together under the banner of Ameritech Business Network. Services ranged from large-scale digital systems with the ability to transmit voice and data simultaneously to a service designed to bring competitively priced digital transmission to customers in smaller markets.

Ameritech Publishing introduced two new programs during 1985, Senior Savings™ and Travel Pages. Senior Savings, offered to Ameritech Yellow Pages buyers, let businesses announce senior citizen discounts and special services by including the Senior Savings logo in their Ameritech Bell Yellow Pages ads. This allowed the Yellow Pages to reach both regular customers and senior citizens with ads in one directory. With Travel Pages Ameritech Publishing took its first step toward a nationwide product. Travel Pages featured articles on travel and leisure activities in each state plus a variety of other information aimed at travelers. It was to be published on a semi-annual basis in each state Ameritech serves.

Ameritech Mobile Communications more than doubled its customer base to over 36,000 cellular customers. It also doubled the number of markets it served, to eight from four, during the year. A new product was also offered—cellular data transmission—which allowed customers to send and receive data between their cellular phones and remote data bases.

1986

Ameritech had another profitable year in 1986. Revenues were up 3.8 percent to $9.4 billion; net income was up 5.6 percent to $1.14 billion; and return on equity climbed to 14.9 percent from 14.7 percent the year before. As good as these numbers were they would have been better if it weren't for refunds, credits and rate reductions in three of the five Bell companies' states.

Through dividends and stock-price appreciation, the value of a shareowner investment had grown by over 150 percent since divestiture. Reflecting confidence in the future, Ameritech declared a three-for-two stock split and raised the dividend twice during the year.

Keeping their word, none of Ameritech's Bell companies sought to increase earnings through higher prices for local telephone service. Revenue growth during the year came from data and voice transmission, access to the network by long distance companies, growth in customer lines and increased business by the unregulated companies.

Revenues from the unregulated companies, including the recently acquired Applied Data Research (ADR), were over $875 million during the year. These companies achieved a 58 percent growth in revenues as opposed to a 26 percent growth in revenues during the previous year. Clearly, however, the five Bell companies were the primary reasons for Ameritech's solid financial position. They generated over 90 percent of the company's total revenue during the year amidst expectations of steady growth in the future.

Keeping an eye to future opportunities the company transferred some 2,500 operator services employees back to Ameritech from AT&T during the year. It was anticipated that this action, while not obviously consistent with a tight expense control policy, would ultimately generate savings of over $40 million a year by internally providing these services in lieu of paying someone else to provide them.

During 1986, the first stand-alone contract negotiations were held between Ameritech and its labor unions. The final contracts contained innovative provisions such as an incentive plan for non-management employees that allowed all employees to share in the company's future success. Across all its companies basic wages increased about five percent a year over the three-year life of the contracts.

During the year Ameritech became the first U.S. regional communications company to be listed on the Tokyo Stock

Exchange. Japan is viewed as a growing source of equity capital, a market for ADR software products, and Ameritech was pursuing other potential business opportunities there as well.

1987

Early in the year Ameritech exercised a major reorganization of its regulated and unregulated enterprises. On the first of February Ormand J. Wade, president of Illinois Bell, became president of Ameritech Bell Group responsible for the five Bell companies, Ameritech Communications, and Ameritech Services. On the same date Robert L. Barnett, president of Wisconsin Bell, became president of the Ameritech Enterprise Group responsible for Ameritech Credit, Ameritech Mobile, Ameritech Publishing and ADR.

Continuing to build on the successes of earlier years Ameritech had its best year yet in 1987. Revenues increased a modest 1.9 percent to over $9.5 billion, but net income grew 4.4 percent to almost $1.2 billion. Based on the solid earnings per share growth, up 7.6 percent to $8.47 per share, the Board of Directors raised the dividend to $5.40 per share.

The tenth edition of the Pan American Games was held in Indianapolis, Indiana, in August of 1987. As the official communications company for the games Ameritech was able to showcase its technological strength to the world. More than 4,000 athletes from 38 countries participated, with almost a million spectators attending and many more millions viewing the games on television around the world.

During the year the company began deployment of another new technology, Signaling System 7. This powerful technology permits virtually unlimited high-speed communications between central offices, computers and other network elements. It lowers costs and increases network flexibility while giving customers greater control over their communications systems.

Ameritech Publishing saw revenue growth of 13 percent from the publication and distribution of 35 million copies of its nearly 500 Ameritech PagesPlus directories and other specialty directories. In the international market Ameritech Publishing established a five year agreement with Nippon Telephone and Telegraph in Japan to publish English language directories in Osaka and Tokyo.

At Applied Data Research revenues grew by 30 percent during the year. ADR's international operations, which served customers in 40 nations, saw revenues up 42 percent over 1986. Also during the year several new products were introduced. eMAIL-VOICE was the first software system to provide both text and voice information delivery to any computer workstation or telephone from corporate data bases.

1988

Ameritech's stated financial goals were to average six to eight percent annual growth in earnings per share over time, to produce 16 to 17 percent return on equity, and to maintain a strong cash flow to generate the maximum capacity for new investments. Results during the year were in line with these goals. Adjusting for the two-for-one stock split in December of 1988, earnings per share increased 7.3 percent, net income was up 4.1 percent and return on equity was at 15.8 percent.

Growth at the Ameritech Bell group was reflected in the addition of 375,000 access lines to its network during the year. This represented an overall growth rate of 2.5 percent— the largest in the company's history—with the rate of growth in business lines at 7.4 percent. Individual business lines generate approximately three times the revenue of residence lines and thus contribute greatly to the company's net income.

Modernization of the network continued during the year with nearly $2 billion invested in network improvements. Approximately one-half of this amount was for state-of-the-art electronic digital switching and fiber-optic transmission systems. Network access minutes increased by 15.6 percent while toll messages grew 5.7 percent.

Ameritech's revenue growth for the year also reflected the higher business levels for the Ameritech Enterprise Group companies. Ameritech Mobile Communications experienced a

68 percent increase in cellular lines to over 146,000 while also expanding its geographical coverage by 17 percent.

Recognizing marketplace opportunities Ameritech sold its 17 percent stake in Cantel for $85 million, producing an after tax gain of $42 million. The Cantel investment had served the strategic purpose of giving Ameritech broader experience in the emerging cellular industry.

The ability to recognize marketplace realities is also a necessary part of a healthy business. Recognizing the lack of tangible synergies being developed between its systems software and communications, the company sold Applied Data Research to Computer Associates International for $170 million.

Still, other new opportunities presented themselves during the year, one being the acquisition of the Tigon Corporation. Tigon was one of the nation's largest voice messaging services and thus provided an extensive foothold in that expanding market. Tigon also operated in the United Kingdom and Japan.

1989

During the year the Ameritech Management Committee was created to replace the former Office of the Chairman. William P. Vititoe, the former president of Michigan Bell, was named the Enterprise Group president, replacing Ormand J. Wade who was named vice chairman. Additionally, Louis J. Rutigliano, the former president of Wisconsin Bell, was named executive vice president of corporate strategy. Remaining in their former positions were William L. Weiss as chairman and chief executive officer, Robert L. Barnett as Bell Group president and William H. Springer as vice chairman and chief financial and administrative officer. The Management Committee was charged to establish the overall vision, mission and strategy for the corporation.

By providing innovative solutions to customers' information needs, Ameritech had by now led the other BHCs in return to equity for six consecutive years. During this period the return to equity increased from 14.3 percent to 15.8 percent while earnings per share averaged an annual growth rate of 6.3 percent. During 1989 earnings per share were $4.59 compared to $4.55 in the previous year.

Growth continued at Ameritech with total revenues up 3.1 percent to $10.2 billion in 1989. The driver of this growth was the continued demand for telecommunications and related services. Customer lines grew by 430,000 to almost sixteen million lines. The ever-important business line growth was up by 7.7 percent with residence growth at 1.4 percent. Toll message use of the network rose 3.8 percent while network access minutes rose by over nine percent.

At Ameritech Mobile, the number of mobile lines grew by 65 percent during the year to 242,000. Ameritech Publishing printed more than 27 billion pages, up 2.4 percent. At Ameritech Credit the financing of more than $96 million in new equipment and systems brought its total amount financed to over one-third of a billion dollars since 1984.

Ameritech continued to expand its customer base by helping to make the Great Lakes region a better place in which to live and work, thereby increasing the potential number of users of its services. In 1989 alone the Ameritech Foundation and Ameritech subsidiaries contributed more than $18 million to organizations dedicated to improving the economic and social well being of the region.

1990

For Ameritech, 1990 could best be characterized as a year of expanding horizons both domestically and internationally. The most dramatic event of the year occurred when Ameritech linked up with Bell Atlantic to purchase the Telecom Corporation of New Zealand, that country's state-owned telecommunications company.

This was simply the largest overseas venture by anyone in the industry since divestiture and significantly expanded Ameritech's participation in global telecommunications. With a purchase price of almost 1.2 billion dollars Ameritech would own nearly 25 percent of the Telecom Corporation in New Zealand. Because Telecom is largely deregulated it would provide a unique opportunity for Ameritech to develop new information technologies that can eventually benefit all its customers as Ameritech continues to seek similar freedoms in the United States.

Growth in its business in America continued to be strong during the year for Ameritech. Now serving more than 16 million business and residential telephone access lines, the company sought to expand its foundation telephone business. A new generation of Custom Calling features was first introduced in Indiana during the year. Features such as Automatic Callback, Repeat Dialing, Call Screening and Distinctive Ringing were successfully trialed in Indiana, then introduced in other states.

American consumers continued to demand their communications systems provide greater mobility and portability. During the year, Ameritech Mobile logged their 325,000th cellular customer. New and enhanced services include an ability for customers to receive their cellular calls in more than 325 cities in the United States and Canada. Also, customers could order new services at sources as diverse as full-service dealers to retailers such as Silo stores to factory-installed phones at Chrysler and Ford dealers throughout the Ameritech region.

While the blockbuster New Zealand acquisition was the top international activity during the year other acquisitions also took place. Ameritech Publishing acquired German industrial Yellow Pages publisher Wer Liefert Was? of Hamburg. The firm—the name of which translates into English as Who Supplies What?—was the leading publisher in the German market with an edition in Austria and one planned in Switzerland.

1991

Ameritech forged ahead in the international marketplace during the year as the initial success of the New Zealand venture became apparent. Ameritech recorded an after-tax gain of over $73 million from the initial public offering of shares in the New Zealand company. When all share sales were complete Ameritech would continue to own almost 25 percent of the company.

Ameritech was also selected as a partner along with the Polish Post Telegraph and France Telecom to construct and operate a nationwide cellular system for Poland. Initial service from this cellular system was to become available in mid-1992 in the capital city of Warsaw. When the system is complete Ameritech will own approximately 25 percent of the company. Clearly, the experience and success Ameritech had gained from its own cellular operations contributed to its being selected for this venture.

When Ameritech customers arrive overseas they are able to use familiar voice-messaging services thanks to Tigon's global network. Ameritech's Tigon Corporation is one of the world's largest voice-mail service bureaus. Its service is available throughout Canada, France, Germany, Italy, the Netherlands, Spain, Switzerland, Sweden, the United Kingdom, Japan, Australia, Taiwan and the United States.

Beyond its global growth Ameritech continued to take care of business at home. In response to a sluggish U.S. economy the company took aggressive steps to stimulate revenues and reduce expenses. During the year revenues climbed to over $10.8 billion while net income was off to $1.165 billion. The decline in net income was largely due to the effect of a special restructuring charge of $141 million. The restructuring charge, without which net income would have gone up during the year, was attributable to multiple reasons. Chief among them were write-downs of assets and intangibles related to the company's unregulated operations, charges for workforce reductions (2,100 employees voluntarily left the company) and the early retirement of debt. While decisions to take a restructuring charge are difficult in the short-term they are often very positive when a long-term view is taken.

Long-term views are also needed in building the network of the future. By the end of 1991 Ameritech's Bell companies had over 400,000 miles of fiber cable in place, compared to only 77,000 miles in 1985. The cellular network also grew with the acquisition of the Cybertel Corporation, which gave Ameritech a cellular license in St. Louis; Ameritech Mobile ended the year serving some 483,000 cellular customers.

1992

With earnings at record levels Ameritech elected to take a non-cash accounting charge of $1.8 billion in 1992. This charge was to cover accounting changes for retirement benefits for current and future retirees. Without this charge the company would have recorded a net income increase of 15 percent over 1991 to $1.3 billion.

Meanwhile, the number of customer access lines in service rose above 17 million and the number of cellular subscribers increased by 22 percent during the year. To provide customers with continued world class service the company continued to investment heavily in its networks—both wireline and wireless.

Ameritech's vision of the future sees a radically different operational environment than existed in 1992. 1993 is seen as the threshold of that future, a future in which there will be no telephone companies as they exist today. Looking inward, Ameritech began working towards a new organization predicated on the tenet that the customer is paramount.

Ameritech began moving towards this new structure by making major organizational changes. Three of the company's vice chairmen unceremoniously retired. Companywide 3,000 employees were removed from the payroll through voluntary early retirement and involuntary termination actions.

William L. Weiss, Ameritech's chairman and CEO, said of the future, "These are difficult times, challenging times, times of historic change. They require us to move in directions that depart from cherished tradition. I am especially grateful for the dedicated employees who have ensured, and continue to ensure, that we will succeed (and) for our customers who are the reason we exist."

11

Bell Atlantic

Bell Atlantic began business as the union of the Bell Telephone Company of Pennsylvania, New Jersey Bell Telephone Company, the Diamond State Telephone Company, and the Chesapeake and Potomac Telephone Company. These companies represented the divested telephone and Yellow Pages operations in the states of New Jersey, Pennsylvania, Delaware, Maryland, Virginia, West Virginia and the District of Columbia.

1984

Thomas E. Bolger, Bell Atlantic's first chairman and CEO, reported in 1984 that the company made substantial progress toward meeting its two primary goals: to provide customers with high-value communications services and to reward investors with increased value in their investments.

A major accomplishment during the year was the formation of the Bell Atlantic Enterprises Group, consisting of seven operating subsidiaries engaged in the sale or lease of communications equipment, the provision of mobile communications and paging services, and the provision of computer service and maintenance.

This group was built through growth and acquisitions including TriContinental Leasing Corporation, which principally leased computers and office automation systems. The Sorbus Service company was acquired to provide customers a source for designing, financing, and servicing communications and information-transport systems.

For people on the move, Bell Atlantic Mobile Systems introduced cellular service in Washington, D.C., Baltimore, Philadelphia, Pittsburgh, northern New Jersey and metropolitan New York City during 1984. Bell Atlantic also acquired A Beeper Company, which provided customers with paging service in 60 markets throughout the United States.

During the year Bell Atlantic's telephone companies invested nearly one billion dollars in fiber optic systems, digital transmission systems and stored program control switching systems. The result of investments such as these is improved service quality and an ever-widening variety of services delivered in the most cost-effective manner.

1985

In 1985 Bell Atlantic continued to make good on its pledge to improve the real value of the company. Net income rose from $973 million in 1984 to almost $1.1 billion, an increase of over 12 percent. Correspondingly, earnings per share jumped a full dollar to $10.94 from $9.94.

The economy of the region served by Bell Atlantic's Network Services companies, composed of Bell of Pennsylvania, Diamond State Telephone, New Jersey Bell and the Chesapeake and Potomac Telephone Company, continued its strong growth. Key measurements such as access lines gained, volume of toll calls and new business development all attested to Bell Atlantic's traditional region being one of the nation's fastest growing areas. For example, access lines served grew by over 400,000 to total over 15 million while toll messages grew by almost 60 million to total nearly two billion.

Modernization of and enhancements to the network continued at a fast pace during 1985. Under the court mandate of equal access the company was supposed to have a third of its access lines converted by September 1, but actually reached 40 percent by that date. By the end of the year over 47 percent of its access lines had been converted. Also by the end of the year over ten percent of access lines were served by digital switching, a fivefold increase from the year before.

The Bell Atlantic Enterprises companies achieved operating revenues of over $425 million. The fact that the nine companies in the group were either started from scratch or acquired over the previous two years once again showed the remarkable growth of Bell Atlantic.

In the information and communications products and services arena two additional acquisitions were completed during the year to complement the previous year's purchase of Sorbus. The first was MAI Canada, Ltd., which marketed and serviced computers and software throughout Canada. To enter the market for the distribution of information products Bell Atlantic acquired CompuShop in June of 1985. CompuShop provided the company with a national presence in personal computers with over 60 stores throughout the United States.

1986

Any year in which a company has a two-for-one stock split and also raises the dividend has to be a good one. Clearly, this was the case for Bell Atlantic in 1986. For the year the company saw net income up 6.8 percent to $1.2 billion and earnings per share up correspondingly to $5.85 from a restated $5.47 in 1985. Return on equity climbed to 14.3 percent from 14.1 percent in the earlier year.

The transition of Bell Atlantic's telephone companies from regulatory-driven utilities to customer-focused enterprises continued and accelerated. A company initiative resulted in customer requirements and customer behavior being analyzed across all market segments. Bell Atlantic learned not only that business and government customers required more sophisticated and efficient solutions to their communications and information problems, but also obtained critical intelligence on how to meet those needs.

Some large universities and corporations, for example, wanted help in providing their own private phone and data transport systems. Others sought expert advice on the costs and benefits of systems components. Still others wanted to interconnect a wide range of incompatible equipment. Bell

Atlantic backed up its pledge to provide the best service possible by working with customers to solve these diverse, often complex problems.

A sampling of the products and services available from Bell Atlantic and designed to meet customer needs included Centrex, the company's flagship switching service for business customers. Centrex offers a wide variety of software-controlled features, many of which are self-programmable by customers. Additionally, the Public Data Network offers a data communications service designed for the cost-effective transmission of interactive, two-way information over existing telephone lines.

During the year the non-regulated businesses in the Bell Atlantic Enterprises Group were realigned into two sectors, Bell Atlantic Enterprises and Bell Atlantic Investment Development Corporation.

The Bell Atlantic Enterprises sector included: Bell Atlantic TriCon Leasing, which focused on the distribution and financing of computer mainframes; Bell Atlantic Mobile Systems, which was the second largest wireline cellular company in the United States; and Sorbus, which specialized in servicing IBM computer mainframes.

Bell Atlantic Investment Development Corporation was responsible for the acquisition of new businesses and the operations of new companies prior to their transition into appropriate Bell Atlantic operating units. Among the companies included in this sector were A Beeper Company, the paging distributor; CompuShop, the microcomputer chain; and Bell Atlantic Business Supplies, a catalog accessories company.

1987

Recognizing that the telephone network businesses are core to the success of Bell Atlantic the company continued its aggressive construction and modernization program. By the end of 1987 over 93 percent of all access lines were served by computer-controlled central offices, of which almost 30 percent were equipped for digital switching.

The company had 112 central office based local area networks in place. This technology allows Bell Atlantic's customers access to simultaneous transmission of voice and data communications. With such a network in place the company will be well positioned to take advantage of future growth opportunities.

During 1987 innovations at Bell Atlantic included products such as Community Centrex℠, which sold Centrex service to real estate developers for resale to tenants; Class Calling Services, which allowed customers to return missed incoming calls, forward calls to other locations, and reject or trace unwanted calls; and the Public Data Network, which made it easy for customers with a home or business computer to communicate inexpensively with other computers.

Bell Atlantic joined forces with GTE in a new venture, Chesapeake Directory Sales Company, which sold Yellow Pages advertising for the four C&P Telephone Companies. Also, Bell Atlantic Education Services was formed to help computer and information managers capitalize on their investment in information technologies.

Systems integration and telecommunications software were marketed overseas through Bell Atlantic International. Agreements were signed with Siemens and IBM to market custom-designed networks in Europe, and with Telefonica in Spain to provide operating support systems to manage Spain's telecommunications network.

During 1987, growth continued at an exciting pace at the Enterprises companies. Revenues at these companies nearly doubled from $447 million in 1986 to $877 million. These revenues contributed $47 million to Bell Atlantic's earnings for the year, with each company showing a clear profit.

Revenues at Bell Atlantic Mobile Systems climbed to $100 million, up 110 percent from 1986. Revenues per employee were 40 percent higher than the industry average and the customer base grew by 60 percent. During the year seven additional Bell Atlantic Mobile Phone Centers were opened and an aggressive marketing campaign was instituted in the northern New Jersey market.

1988

At the end of 1988 Thomas E. Bolger retired from his position as the first chairman and chief executive officer of Bell Atlantic. Raymond W. Smith was appointed as his successor, first as chief executive officer in 1988 and then as chairman of the board early the next year.

In Mr. Bolger's final year at the helm Bell Atlantic posted strong financial results. Earnings per share were up 6.6 percent to $6.65 from $6.24 in 1987. Dividends reached $4.08 per share, while net income climbed to $1.32 billion and return on equity was up to 14.5 percent.

During the leadership transition Mr. Smith stated that the goal of Bell Atlantic was to be a leading international information and communications company. To accomplish this, he said, "Bell Atlantic will become the premier supplier of communications network and value-added services in its region; a major international provider of high-quality business systems, services, and products, supported by financial services; and a major international developer and distributor of high-value information products."

During 1988 Bell Atlantic continued to focus on being a low cost/high productivity provider. The company was able to increase the number of access lines served per telephone network employee from 178 at divestiture to 224 during 1988. While nationwide the percentage of households having basic telephone service was 92.9, this statistic was a full two points higher at 94.9 percent in Bell Atlantic's region.

In March of 1988, when a federal court in Washington, D.C. authorized the transportation of information services by the BHCs, Bell Atlantic acted immediately. In May, Bell Atlantic began offering two message storage services in Washington, D.C. These were a real estate service which allowed house-hunters to call for recorded messages about available properties, and the Federal Voting Assistance Program which gave overseas military personnel access to messages recorded by political candidates for the 1988 elections. Services such as these and others held the potential for greatly contributing to future revenue streams.

The corporation also kept an eye to the future in the international arena. While legal and regulatory barriers remained solid in domestic markets, Bell Atlantic perceived more freedom in international markets. This led the corporation to establish Bell Atlantic Customer Services International, Bell Atlantic Financial Overseas Corporation and Bell Atlantic International. These companies were prepared to capitalize on opportunities that would be created in 1992 and beyond, when the 12-nation European Community would become, in effect, a single economic market.

1989

During the year revenue growth was strong, as were the underlying business volumes throughout Bell Atlantic. Revenues climbed to over $11.4 billion from $10.9 billion the year before for a five percent increase. However, net income for the year was down by nearly $250 million because of write-offs and special charges necessary for improving future profitability.

Special charges of $320 million were for the cost of an early retirement program that reduced employment levels by almost 1,700 managers, the funding of a trust for future costs of medical benefits for non-management retirees, the write-down of certain inventories and other assets, and the refinancing of long term debt. This purging set the stage for future opportunities and helped insure the quality of future earnings. The investment community recognized the long-term strength of Bell Atlantic by increasing the stock price by 50 percent during the year.

In 1989, Bell Atlantic's telephone companies continued their progress toward building an all-digital fiber network. During the year $2.3 billion was invested to maintain and upgrade network facilities. Improvements included adding 100,000 miles of fiber to the 314,000 miles already in place, and increasing from 56 to 66 percent the ratio of digital switching offices in the region.

The intelligence of the network is found in Signalling System 7 (SS7), a technology that allows telephone switches to exchange information about calls at high rates of speed. SS7 enhances effective use of network circuits and enriches the variety of services with offerings such as Caller ID, Call Block and Return Call. These features provide customers the services they want and also stimulate the growth of the basic telephone business.

Revenues from the unregulated side of the business continued to climb during the year. Non-network revenues rose almost 17 percent and totaled some $1.35 billion, compared to $1.15 billion during 1988. Contributing substantially to this growth was the continued success of Bell Atlantic Mobile Systems, where the number of customers was up 88 percent over the previous year's total, and the financial and real estate holding companies, where revenues were up some $125 million for the year.

Other highlights for the year included the evolution of Sorbus as it maintained its status as the world's largest independent computer maintenance company. The acquisition of Control Data Corporation's independent maintenance division in the U.S. and Canada was completed early in 1990. With this acquisition Sorbus became the leader for independent DEC maintenance, a position it already held with respect to IBM computers.

1990

Bell Atlantic began its seventh year of operations with another two-for-one stock split and a 7.3 percent dividend increase. These were sure signs Bell Atlantic was returning to the growth stage that had been the key characteristic of its first five years as a stand-alone company.

During the second quarter of 1990 Bell Atlantic took two giant steps forward in the international arena. The first step was joining with Ameritech and two New Zealand firms to purchase Telecom Corporation of New Zealand. Bell Atlantic invested $1.2 billion in this partnership and would end up with approximately 25 percent ownership of the New Zealand tele-phone company. Next, Bell Atlantic teamed up with U S WEST to win a joint bid to build a wireless communications network and a packet-switched data network in Czechoslovakia.

The acquisition of New Zealand Telecom provided strategic positioning for future opportunities in the Pacific Rim as well as revenue growth opportunities. The Czechoslovakian project provided Bell Atlantic a high visibility base in Europe in addition to the growth opportunity in wireless communica-tions. All in all, these two projects will contribute substantially to the development of Bell Atlantic's international business.

In addition, the company's domestic network services operations were far from idle during the year. C&P Telephone Company completed the first phase of the Washington Interagency Telecommunications System. This system will ultimately connect 130,000 employees at 64 agencies in and around Washington, D.C. through an advanced fiber optic net-work. Bell Atlantic also signed its 100,000th customer for Answer Call less than a year after the service was introduced. Answer Call enables customers to leave a standard or personal greeting on their lines and automatically records messages if the line is busy or is not answered.

Maintaining its role as a leading corporate citizen Bell Atlantic and its employees continued to contribute to the com-munity. For instance, Bell of Pennsylvania was recognized by the United Way of Southeastern Pennsylvania for raising more than $1 million from corporate and employee contributions— just one of several Bell Atlantic companies cited by local United Ways for their support. During the year the Bell Atlantic Charitable Foundation pledged almost $300,000 to the Family Literacy Project. The goal of this project is to end inter-generational illiteracy by teaching reading skills to both par-ents and children.

1991

In 1991 Bell Atlantic became the first of the Bell Holding Companies to report a loss from a year of operations. On revenues of over $12 billion the company had a negative net income of almost $225 million. This loss occurred because Bell Atlantic decided to take a one-time, non-cash, after-tax accrual of over $1.5 billion to cover the new accounting standard regarding health and life insurance for retirees. All companies would have to eventually comply with the new standard. Without this one-time special charge Bell Atlantic would have achieved a new record net income (before the special charge) of over $1.33 billion, or $3.41 on a per share basis.

In an attempt to achieve even greater levels of future efficiency the company again offered an early retirement plan to some of its management employees. More than 3,200 employees accepted the offer and the company ended the year with 75,700 employees—a total reduction of almost 6,000 from the year before.

The company also recognized that the performance of its financial services operations, particularly the computer systems leasing and real estate development divisions, were not performing up to Bell Atlantic's standards. Bell Atlantic made the strategic decision to reduce the value on the company's books of those divisions. While these were painful decisions it did show the character of Bell Atlantic to recognize economic realities and to get over the hurdles that stood in its way.

In New Zealand, the initial public offering of shares netted Bell Atlantic a gain of about $75 million. In Czechoslovakia cellular service was inaugurated on the network being built there. A new joint venture was being planned with STET, the Italian telephone company, that would create an advanced strategic software company in Italy. Finally, the European computer maintenance business owned by Bell Atlantic was realigned into a joint venture with International Computers Limited, one of Europe's largest computer firms.

Network Services, the umbrella name for the telephone companies of Bell Atlantic, also ended 1991 in a stronger competitive position. The company won several important government contracts, including one worth more than $600 million over 10 years to modernize the telecommunications system for the U.S. Department of Defense. Taking advantage of favorable market conditions, the company also refinanced and paid off hundreds of millions of dollars worth of both short and long-term debt. Services such as Caller ID and Return Call, voice messaging services such as Answer Call, and data services such as ISDN all experienced tremendous growth in 1991.

1992

Bell Atlantic's revenues for the year modestly nudged up to $12.6 billion from $12.5 billion, reflecting the continued deliberate downsizing of the company's computer leasing and real estate business. However, net income climbed to nearly $1.4 billion for a 12 percent increase over the previous year (before 1991's change in accounting principle).

What used to be called the traditional telephone business continued to be the most dynamic segment of the information industry. Bell Atlantic continued to steadily invest $2 billion a year in building its network. New services such as Caller ID and Return Call combined with well-established products such as Call Waiting to generate over $360 million in revenues by themselves.

On April 30 Bell Atlantic completed its merger with Metro Mobile CTS, Inc. Over 34 million shares of Bell Atlantic common stock was issued to cover the cost of the merger. During the first quarter of the year Bell Atlantic common stock had been trading as high as $49 per share making the cost of Metro Mobile upwards of $1.6 billion.

International partnerships with U S WEST in eastern Europe and with Ameritech in New Zealand continued to grow. The Bell Atlantic international business strategy continued to be one of pursuing opportunities—principally in cellular systems and privatizations—on a highly selective basis.

In stating his outlook for the company's future chairman and CEO Raymond W. Smith stated, "Bell Atlantic intends to compete in this new world the old-fashioned way: by sharpening our market focus, reducing our cost structure, speeding up our response time, and offering the highest-value products and services of any competitor in the business."

12

BellSouth

BellSouth inherited the legacies of the Southern Bell and South Central Bell Telephone companies from AT&T at divestiture. The telephone and Yellow Pages publishing operations in the nine states of Florida, Georgia, North Carolina, South Carolina, Alabama, Kentucky, Louisiana, Mississippi and Tennessee were joined together to form BellSouth.

1984

With $21.5 billion dollars in assets and 13.6 million access lines in service at inception, BellSouth was the largest of the seven newly established regional companies. Growth projections showed that one-third of all growth in the United States would occur in BellSouth's nine state region by the end of the century. With a strong growth forecast linked to the large base of BellSouth operations the company was well positioned to meet the future.

At divestiture John L. Clendenin, BellSouth's first chairman, announced three fundamental strategies to guide the company in the future. Those strategies called for BellSouth to be financially driven while maintaining its traditional emphasis on service; to emphasize telecommunications, the business it knows best; and to pursue orderly diversification.

BellSouth quickly began to fulfill the future promise of those strategies. During 1984 the company saw total revenues of over $9.5 billion and net income in excess of $1.2 billion. On a per share basis this amounted to earnings of $4.28 and allowed the company to declare dividends of $2.60 per share.

At the same time results from customer surveys and internal quality measurements confirmed the commitment to excellent service.

The emphasis on telecommunications was evident from the corporation's successes in meeting a broad range of service obligations. For instance, the company made substantial progress in the implementation of equal access. Forecasts showed that by the middle of 1985 the company would have converted over half its customer lines to equal access, well above the court mandated 33 percent level. Also the number of customer access lines in service rose by over 400,000 to top 14 million; at the same time the number of employees per 10,000 access lines shrank to 68 from 73.

The orderly diversification strategy was evidenced by the launching of several new subsidiaries. BellSouth Advertising & Publishing expanded into specialized directories and the provision of directory publishing services to other telephone companies. The cellular subsidiary, BellSouth Mobility, began operations in Miami in May of 1984 and by the following January was also serving New Orleans, Atlanta and Louisville. At BellSouth Advanced Systems, the equipment sales subsidiary, the company exceeded projected first year operating results.

The 96,000 employees of BellSouth experienced an inaugural year in which change was constant, yet the company continued to pursue its vision of being a financially driven, service oriented telecommunications company. Despite legislative, regulatory and judicial challenges BellSouth made 1984 the cornerstone of its future.

1985

BellSouth Corporation's performance in 1985 surpassed that of its successful first year. Earnings per share increased to $4.69, an improvement of 9.6 percent over the previous year. Return to equity was 14.4 percent which reflected continued progress towards earnings objectives. Net income was $1.4 billion on revenues of almost $10.7 billion; these figures were up 12.8 percent and 10.7 percent respectively over 1984.

Reflecting confidence in the future of BellSouth the stock price gained over 40 percent for the year to reach a high of $49 per share compared to a high of $35.50 in 1984. Also during the year the dividend grew from $2.60 to $2.80 per share.

The nine-state BellSouth region continued to enjoy healthy economic and population growth trends. Economists projected continued large employment gains for the region on the order of one million new jobs in 1986 and 1987, with real income growing faster than the national rate.

During the year the telephone operations at Southern Bell and South Central Bell combined to add nearly 500,000 new access lines, raising the total in service to well over 14.5 million. By the end of 1985 equal access had been furnished to over 60 percent of the lines in BellSouth's region.

Southern Bell and South Central Bell continued to integrate enhanced technology into the BellSouth network at a pacesetting rate. During 1985, the BellSouth operating companies installed 57,000 miles of fiber optic cable, doubling the amount in place in 1984. This enabled BellSouth to lead the industry in fiber optic cable installed. BellSouth also began to test ISDN in preparation for the next expansion of the telephone's role at home and at work.

By the end of the year BellSouth Mobility had added cellular networks in Baton Rouge, Birmingham, Chattanooga, Jacksonville, Memphis, Nashville, Orlando and West Palm Beach. The company also continued to improve other systems, investing almost $20 million to upgrade and expand existing networks in South Florida and Atlanta.

BellSouth International, the corporation's then newest venture, began operations in July of 1985. Headquartered in Atlanta, BellSouth International was charged to manage the corporation's activities outside of the U.S. The immediate focus was on locating telecommunications opportunities in the Pacific Basin and Europe. The company's first overseas office opened in Hong Kong in October 1985.

1986

Building on its successful first two years, the company had another banner year in 1986. Revenues climbed by nearly $800 million to over $11.4 billion. Correspondingly, net income was up over 12 percent to nearly $1.6 billion. On a per share basis earnings were up from $4.70 to $5.07 and the dividend jumped from $2.80 per share to $3.06. These financial accomplishments seemed to bear testimonial proof of the successful implementation of BellSouth's business strategy.

On January 1, 1986, all nonregulated subsidiaries were consolidated under the direction of BellSouth Enterprises. The motivation behind this move was to promote market development, manage resource allocation and to ensure profitable growth. William O. McCoy was named president of BellSouth Enterprises in addition to his position as vice chairman of BellSouth.

By the end of 1986 BellSouth Enterprises had been organized into three operating units. These included the Communications Systems Group, the Corporate Enterprises Group and the Advertising and Publishing Group. By the end of the year these organizations, headquartered in Atlanta, employed over 8,600 people and generated in excess of $1.5 billion in annual revenue.

The Communications Systems Group was charged with the management of business communications systems sales for the operating telephone companies, management of multi-user telecommunications systems, and sales of fiber optics systems. Companies in this group included BellSouth Advanced Systems, BellSouth Government Systems, BellSouth Systems Technology and FiberLAN.

The Corporate Enterprises Group was composed of mobile cellular communications services, international business, and real estate operations. The companies in this group were BellSouth Mobility, BellSouth International, Sunlink and American Cellular.

The Advertising and Publishing Group's duties included the publication of white pages, Yellow Pages and specialty

directories, sales of directory advertising for directories published by BellSouth and other companies, publication and
printing of other materials, and graphics and photocomposi-
tion services. Included in this group were BellSouth
Advertising and Publishing, L.M. Berry and Company,
BellSouth Information Systems, Steven Graphics and
TechSouth.

1987

Celebrating the continued success of its operations
BellSouth declared a three-for-two stock split on February 5,
1987. Also during the first quarter the company boosted the
dividend payout from $2.04 to $2.20 per share on an annualized
basis. The year's operating results supported the optimism
behind the decision to split the stock. Revenues increased a
healthy 7.2 percent to over $12.2 billion while net income
reached $1.67 billion, reflecting a 4.8 percent gain over 1985's
outstanding results.

Driven by the robust economy of the Southeast, South
Central Bell and Southern Bell gained more than 650,000
access lines in 1987—28 percent more than the previous year's
record-setting performance. At the same time telephone operations became more efficient through the centralized planning
and support efforts of BellSouth Services. Illustrating this efficiency was the continuing decrease in employees per 10,000
access lines. By the end of 1987 it took approximately 55 hard-
working employees to support 10,000 access lines, down from
65 employees in 1984.

Continuing to upgrade the telephone network was also
a high priority. By the end of 1987 BellSouth had over 200,000
miles of fiber optic cable in place. The conversion of central
offices to electronic switching also continued; by year's end
over 80 percent of South Central Bell's central offices were
electronic (digital and analog), while Southern Bell had converted over 70 percent of its central offices.

BellSouth recognized that leadership in telecommunications would require pursuing opportunities beyond tra-

ditional telephone service and beyond its geographic region. Achieving that leadership goal would demand a global perspective, and in 1987 BellSouth posted successes on several international fronts.

These successes included signing agreements on four continents to expand the communications networks of France, Italy, Guatemala and India, as well as obtaining a majority interest in Australia's largest independent paging and answering service company. The corporation was also a major exhibitor at Telecom '87 in Geneva, Switzerland, the international telecommunications industry's largest and most prestigious gathering. BellSouth shares were now trading on the New York, London and Tokyo stock exchanges; this provided access to the world's major capital markets and raised the visibility of the company in the international financial community.

1988

"By virtually any measure, BellSouth's first five years have been marked by success," claimed John L. Clendenin, BellSouth's chairman and chief executive officer. The continuing increases in revenues, net income and earnings per share in every year since divestiture attested to the accuracy of that comment. After five years of operations BellSouth had evolved into four fundamental operating entities: South Central Bell, Southern Bell, BellSouth Services and BellSouth Enterprises.

South Central Bell is the leading provider of telecommunications products and services in Alabama, Kentucky, Louisiana, Mississippi and Tennessee. During 1988 South Central Bell installed the nation's first Common Channel Signaling System 7 to provide advanced network services in Memphis, Tennessee. The company also served the Republican National Convention in New Orleans, providing over 5,000 temporary service lines for that event.

South Central Bell took the lead in the FCC-approved recombination of BellSouth's equipment and network marketing forces with a trial in Mississippi. South Central Bell also achieved 100 percent of its service objectives at the company and state levels, underscoring its commitment to putting the customer first.

Southern Bell provides local exchange, information access, exchange access and intraLATA long-distance services in major parts of Florida, Georgia and North and South Carolina, which together constitute one of the nation's fastest growing regions. In 1988, the company enjoyed its third straight year of record growth in access lines, invested $1.75 billion in network enhancements, and remained a world leader in the application of fiber optic cable with nearly a quarter of a million miles installed.

BellSouth Services is jointly owned by South Central Bell and Southern Bell and performs staff and planning functions for both. These services provide a common focus and a standard operating environment for their regulated telephone businesses.

BellSouth Enterprises was formed in 1986 to pursue orderly business development outside the arena of traditional telephone service. Most of the work of BellSouth Enterprises is in four major lines of business: directory advertising and publishing, mobile communications, marketing and business development (including international activities), and telecommunications systems sales and computer systems leasing and maintenance.

1989

Continuing the strong growth of the first five years, BellSouth posted outstanding results in 1989. For the first time revenues topped the $14 billion mark while net income climbed to over $1.7 billion. On a per share basis earnings were at $3.64 for the year, up almost four percent. The value of BellSouth's assets exceeded $30 billion for the first time.

Beginning in 1989 a new era in sophistication was introduced through TouchStar® services. Included in the TouchStar package are services such as Call Tracing, Call Blocking and Call Selector. These services add value for the home customer in saving time and money while improving peace of mind.

In the workplace, BellSouth continued to recognize the needs of businesses both large and small. The family of products and services offered by BellSouth includes private branch exchange (PBX) systems and central office based ESSX® service. ESSX service performs functions similar to most PBX systems, except it is based in the local exchange central office, not on the customer's premises. This way, as small businesses grow, their telecommunications systems can also grow to meet the needs of the business.

For large business customers, the BellSouth National Accounts program was established. Whether the customer's needs are local or national in scope, account managers can bring all of the resources of BellSouth to solve the customer's problem.

Across the nation BellSouth continued to enlarge its profile, acquiring Mobile Communications Corporation of America (MCCA) for $710 million in April. This catapulted BellSouth into prominence as one of the nation's largest providers of paging and cellular service. With over 400,000 cellular customers and over 800,000 paging customers across the U.S. the company was well positioned to enjoy the future growth of wireless communications.

During the year BellSouth also continued to grow from an international perspective, heading a consortium of six companies in introducing South America's first private cellular mobile communications network in Argentina. On November 1, 1989, only 14 months after the consortium was awarded the contract, the cellular network introduced service for its first customers. In Europe BellSouth joined with five other companies to provide a much needed paging system to link travelers as they cross the borders between the United Kingdom, Germany, Italy and France.

1990

During 1990 BellSouth experienced its first stumble in the growth of net income. While revenues grew by $350 million to over $14.3 billion, net income was off some $110 million to $1.6 billion. Part of this was attributable to "givebacks" to state regulatory commissions in exchange for a more realistic and potentially more profitable incentive regulation. Costs were also incurred as the companies of BellSouth became leaner through an early retirement program in which nearly 1,150 managers participated. Finally, the company refinanced some high interest debt and wrote off some underperforming computer leasing portfolios.

Despite this slight setback, the company continued to grow the fundamentals of the business. The number of access lines that South Central Bell and Southern Bell had in service by the end of 1990 stood at 17.5 million—up by some 500,000 over 1989. Of these lines almost 13 million were under some form of progressive incentive regulation. In six states out of BellSouth's traditional nine state region some form of shared earnings plan between customers and shareholders was in place. The bridge between the past world of monopoly and the new world of competition was being built.

In the wireless arena the growth of the customer base continued at a tremendous pace. The number of paging customers was up over 40,000 for the year, with 860,000 customers in place. The number of cellular customers grew by almost 250,000 to end the year with 680,000 customers. Products such as voice mail, mobile fax service and data terminals allowed customers to use their cars as their offices, and also helped grow BellSouth revenues.

During 1990 BellSouth had a growing presence in the international marketplace. One BellSouth-led consortium secured the non-wireline cellular license in Uruguay while another made progress in securing the second cellular license in Venezuela. In Australia, application was made to become the second nationwide telecommunications company, while in neighboring New Zealand the company was awarded a license to build a cellular system.

1991

In 1991 BellSouth implemented the findings of a comprehensive analysis of its telephone operations. On March 1 all telephone-related companies—Southern Bell, South Central Bell and BellSouth Services—were realigned into a unified new structure. This new structure, known as BellSouth Telephone Operations, was designed to enhance the company's ability to deliver efficient and effective customer-focused services in the telecommunications marketplace. B. Franklin Skinner, who formerly headed Southern Bell, was named the company's first chairman and CEO. F. Duane Ackerman, who formerly headed South Central Bell, was named president and chief operating officer.

During the year BellSouth committed itself to the future of wireless data networks. These networks may be thought of as being to computers what cellular is to phones. Work was initiated to join with the RAM Broadcasting Corporation to own and operate mobile data communications networks worldwide. The venture would require a $300 million investment to open up the network, justified with 10 million potential customers in the U.S. alone.

In the international arena BellSouth decided to invest up to $300 million in a consortium that was awarded an unprecedented license to become the second Australian telecommunications company. This company would cover all aspects of telecommunications including wireline, wireless and satellite.

BellSouth also continued to take the steps necessary to drive down the cost of doing business as more than 4,000 managers took advantage of an early retirement program during the year. The company took a one-time charge of $70 million to implement the plan, but the future savings resulting from the reduction in staff will continue to pay large dividends far into the future.

At the same time the corporation continued to grow the core telephone business. Through 1991 BellSouth had sold some 1.9 million TouchStar features such as Caller ID. Also during the year the one millionth customer line was connected with BellSouth's central office-based ESSX service. The continued development of products such as the Advanced Intelligent Network will create future revenue opportunities while providing further customized service to meet each user's specific needs.

1992

In the fall of 1992 Hurricane Andrew slammed into BellSouth's primary operational territory. From Florida to Louisiana Andrew's 140 mile-per-hour wrath was the most devastating storm in U.S. history. Despite the horrific suffering and over $30 billion in property damage the BellSouth telephone network continued to serve the needs of its customers.

BellSouth's strategy to keep its network up and running had been years in the making. Central offices had been fortified, fiber optic cable was buried and emergency procedures were in place. As a result, not one of Southern Bell's major central offices went out of service during the storm's fury, and not a single south Florida E911 center lost service.

From a business perspective 1992 was equally impressive. Rebounding from the previous year operating revenues topped the $15 billion level for the first time. Net income climbed to over $1.6 billion and on a per share basis earnings rose to $3.30 from $3.04.

Cellular was the fastest growing segment of BellSouth's business. Worldwide wireless revenues, which include paging, increased 54 percent during the year to nearly $1.2 billion. BellSouth's domestic cellular business grew by 44 percent during the year, serving over 1.1 million customers.

The company's core telephone operations also continued to grow. What was already the nation's largest base of domestic access lines in service grew by over 600,000 to eighteen million. Also by the end of 1992 over half a million MemoryCall® voice mailboxes were in service, more than double the previous year's total.

International growth continued during the year as well.

In Australia BellSouth's Optus Communications consortium began offering analog cellular service in June 1992. Optus gained about 400 customers every business day, with its digital network becoming operational in 1993. In early 1993 BellSouth's consortium was awarded a license to compete in the German cellular market.

John L. Clendenin, the chairman, president and CEO of BellSouth, summed up BellSouth's commitment to leadership when he said, "The pace of change in this business is astounding. You can watch the changes and see what happens, or you can make the changes happen. We're making them happen."

13

NYNEX

The name NYNEX was taken from the market the corporation serves. "NY" stands for New York, "NE" for New England and "X" for the undefined prospects of the future. NYNEX was formed at divestiture by the merger of the New England and New York telephone companies, including the regulated telephone and Yellow Pages operations in the states of Massachusetts, Vermont, New Hampshire, Rhode Island, Maine, New York and a small portion of Connecticut.

1984

At the time of divestiture a strong economic recovery was in progress in the Northeastern U.S. One-fifth of the nation's Fortune 500 firms are headquartered in the primary markets NYNEX serves. The combination of these two factors provided the ideal conditions for NYNEX to begin operations.

NYNEX started business with an asset base in excess of $18.5 billion that grew to over $19.8 billion by the end of the year. Revenues were over $9.5 billion with net income being almost $1 billion. On a per share basis earnings stood at over $10.00 and the dividend for the year was $6.00 per share.

At New England Telephone, headquartered in Boston, the number of access lines grew by 167,000 to a total of 4.6 million lines. During the year the company handled 63 million originating calls per business day. To ensure continued growth 14,000 miles of fiber cable were installed in 1984 while 15 new digital switching centers were brought on-line.

New York Telephone, headquartered in New York City,

saw an increase in the number of access lines of 201,000 to a total of 8.6 million. The company handled 94 million originating calls per business day during the year. Some 12,000 miles of fiber optic cable were installed and 18 more digital switching stations were brought on-line.

In 1984, NYNEX Mobile Communications introduced cellular service in New York City and Boston. NYNEX Information Resources published 285 telephone directories with a circulation of 26 million copies. NYNEX Business Information Systems was formed to market network services, voice and data PBX systems, and integrated office systems.

D. C. Staley, the corporation's first chairman, said the market NYNEX serves, "is a marketplace far too vast for any single observer to claim the vision to encompass it all." He also stated, "the mission of NYNEX is to anticipate and to serve enough of the tremendous potential in the marketplace to make NYNEX a recognized leader in the information industry."

1985

Measuring 1985 against the benchmark year of 1984 illustrated the success of NYNEX's operations. For the year operating revenues posted a 7.7 percent increase to over $10.3 billion. Net income was up over $100 million to almost $1.1 billion, representing earnings per share of $10.85 with a declared annual dividend of $6.40.

During the year NYNEX focused not only on growing the numbers, but also on growing the business by aggressively entering the retail sales market with its Datago℠ Business Centers. These retail outlets offered computers, copiers and office security systems. By the end of the year NYNEX was operating eleven stores throughout the northeastern U.S. Also during the year NYNEX acquired Computer Solutions and combined it with the Datago Business Centers. This acquisition provided an immediate presence in the Syracuse and Endwell, N.Y. markets.

Expansion was also underway at NYNEX Mobile Communications, the cellular mobile telephone subsidiary.

During 1985 service was introduced in several major northeastern cities: Boston, Worcester, and New Bedford-Fall River, Massachusetts; Albany, New York, and Providence, Rhode Island. The New Bedford-Fall River cellular system was the 100th cellular system to begin operations in the United States.

At NYNEX Information Resources, NYNEX's publishing company, new product development contributed to its continuing success as the premier source of directories in the markets NYNEX serves. Spanish Yellow Pages were made available for the Hispanic communities in New Jersey as well as New York City. Also, the company was granted permission to produce its first non-directory product, *Changing Homes* magazine. This magazine focused on the needs of newly-moved households.

At the core telephone operations of New York Telephone and New England Telephone the pace of growth also intensified. Installed fiber optic cable was up about 50 percent to over 74,000 miles. Also during the year 66 new digital switching centers were brought on-line. This represented an increase of over 150 percent in the number of customers served by digital lines.

With the information industry rapidly evolving into a global marketplace, NYNEX established the NYNEX International Company. NYNEX representatives traveled to the Far East, South America and Europe to meet with government and industry leaders. This was a recognition that NYNEX must pursue ventures at home and abroad that enhance the future potential value of the corporation.

1986

To say that in 1986 NYNEX achieved impressive operating results would be a major understatement. For the year revenues increased by over $1 billion to exceed $11.3 billion, while net income was up by $120 million to over $1.2 billion. These figures represented increases of 10 percent and 11 percent respectively over 1985's performance.

With the price of NYNEX common stock on the New York Stock Exchange hovering around $100 the company declared a two-for-one stock split on March 20, 1986. At the same time, the dividend was increased by almost nine percent to $3.48 a share after the split. By the third quarter of the year the price of a share was back up to more than $70. Clearly, Wall Street and the company's stockholders were excited about the growth at NYNEX.

Building on the Datago Business Centers' growth NYNEX decided to establish NYNEX Business Centers as a nationwide presence. During the year the number of new Business Centers was up sharply to a total of 94 outlets. These stores were operating in 33 states and the District of Columbia, offering customers one-stop shopping for telecommunications and computer equipment and networking know-how.

By the end of 1986 the number of NYNEX's principal subsidiaries stood at ten. Other subsidiaries, in addition to those mentioned earlier, included: NYNEX Credit Company, which provided financing assistance to customers who made telecommunications purchases from both NYNEX and non-NYNEX companies; NYNEX Properties Company, which provided real estate expertise as the broker and developer for the NYNEX family of companies; and NYNEX Material Enterprises, which offered procurement and support services to the NYNEX family of companies.

New ventures set up to explore NYNEX's future possibilities included teaming up with Citicorp and RCA/GE to form CNR Partners which carried out market research in areas such as the future of home banking. NYNEX also became a 50 percent partner with Cable and Wireless of England to explore the possibility of constructing and operating a trans-Atlantic fiber cable. In order to fully explore international possibilities, NYNEX International Company opened up offices in Hong Kong and in Geneva, Switzerland during the year.

1987

In 1987 NYNEX once again posted impressive operating results. During the year revenues climbed over $700 million to almost $12.1 billion, and net income climbed over $60 million to $1.27 billion. On a per share basis earnings climbed 25 cents to $6.26 while dividends were increased by about four percent to $3.80.

At the core telephone operations of NYNEX the growth was equally strong. A gain of over 450,000 access lines was recorded so that by the end of the year the total number of customer access lines stood at 14.4 million. To meet present and future customer needs NYNEX invested over $2.3 billion during the year to improve the networks of New England Telephone and New York Telephone.

The commitment to maintaining and enhancing the network means replacing older electromechanical technology with the latest digital and fiber optic technology. During the year the number of digital access lines increased to more than 3.5 million and over 195,000 miles of fiber optic cable were installed at NYNEX's telephone operations.

The NYNEX telephone companies continued to add new features to the network to provide greater service potential to their customers. Services such as INTELLIPATH II[SM] Digital Centrex were introduced during 1987 to assist customers by providing a network alternative to customer-owned telephone equipment. During 1987 over 95,000 INTELLIPATH II lines were installed to provide customers with network-based features such as three-way calling and call transfer.

Historic agreements were reached during 1987 with the regulatory commissions in New York and Vermont. Both accords offered NYNEX greater opportunity to respond to changes in the telecommunications marketplace. These accords also stabilized rates and provided a means for sharing profits with both customers and shareowners.

Other NYNEX companies had a strong year, also. The more than 80 NYNEX Business Centers rose to become one of the top three non-franchise computer-center chains in the nation. In Massachusetts and Rhode Island the directory services company introduced NYNEX BOATERS, a directory targeted toward boat owners, as its first specialty directory. Based on the success of this offering plans were made to produce other maritime advertising directories in New York,

Florida, California and the Pacific Northwest.

1988

NYNEX saw itself evolving from a regional supplier of telephone services to a worldwide provider of telecommunications, information systems, software, publishing and business services. The vision of NYNEX had clearly been broadened and the company had set its sights on becoming a leader in the global information industry.

NYNEX continued to record continuous strong earnings growth year over year. For 1988, the company earned $1.3 billion in net income on revenues of $12.7 billion. On a per share basis earnings were up to $6.63.

NYNEX invested $2.7 billion in modernizing and expanding its network, and the number of customer access lines grew to reach 14.9 million. The number of miles of fiber optic cable in service stood at 295,000, and the network was handling over 182 million calls per business day.

Impressive growth at the other NYNEX companies also continued during the year. At the cellular operations the company now served over 135,000 customers. Not bad for a company that didn't even exist—let alone have any customers—at divestiture. When NYNEX Business Centers began operations in 1986, their goal was to add value by combining networking expertise with hardware and software knowledge. By 1988 these centers had cashed in on that edge, selling nearly $400 million in equipment and services.

Expanding NYNEX's international presence continued to be a top priority. To expand its expertise in banking software NYNEX bought the BIS Group in 1987 and AGS Computers in 1988. Both companies brought close working relationships with major banks in important financial centers. By adding these skills NYNEX became a top supplier of information industry products and systems to banks and other industries around the world. While the international activities were at this point a small part of the NYNEX picture they were to grow larger with every passing day.

1989

If there ever was a year that could be called one of transition 1989 was such a year for NYNEX. The most obvious change happened at the top with the retirement of NYNEX's founding chairman and chief executive officer D. C. "Bud" Staley. After 43 years in the telecommunications industry Mr. Staley retired and was replaced by William C. Ferguson. Part of the transition to new leadership included the early retirement of vice chairman William G. Burns.

While operating revenues increased some $450 million during the year to $13.2 billion, net income was off by more than $500 million to just over $800 million. This decrease was due to many factors including a labor strike, early retirement incentive programs, asset and billing writedowns, and regulatory charges.

On August 5, 1989, the collective bargaining agreements expired with NYNEX's two unions, the CWA and the IBEW, and a work stoppage commenced the next day. A protracted strike continued until December 1989 when the unions ratified new contracts. NYNEX recorded $100 million in expenses for such items as deferred vacation payments, delayed installations and other strike-related matters. Thus, the effects of the lengthy strike took a heavy toll on employees of NYNEX, both management and non-management, as well as on the company's bottom line.

As part of NYNEX's commitment to become more cost-competitive, early retirement programs were offered to management and non-management employees in 1989. By year's end some 1,500 employees had taken the option and another 2,500 were expected do so in early 1990. While in the long-term these programs would increase earnings through lower expense levels, the short-term financial impact was negative; the cost of these programs forced NYNEX to take a charge of approximately $75 million in 1989.

During the year NYNEX also booked charges of over $100 million due to the implementation of a 1987 New York State Public Service Commission decision to reduce local and long distance rates charged by New York Telephone. The rate reductions were made possible by the cost savings from the Tax Reform Act of 1986 and by pension cost reductions.

With the corporation taking so many different charges during the year it decided to take the opportunity to "clean up the balance sheet." NYNEX took additional charges such as writing down the value of excess inventory and writing off the value of accounts receivable that would most likely not be paid. While this action was painful it allowed NYNEX to put a great deal of bad news behind it as it moved into the future.

1990

Despite the beginnings of a severe recession in the Northeast and the lingering effects of 1989's financial charges, NYNEX still moved its key indicators forward in 1990. While revenues for the company were up some three percent for the year, at slightly under $13.6 billion, net income improved by 17 percent to stand at $950 million. Dividends were up 20 cents a share to $4.56 while earnings per share stood at $4.78.

During 1990 it was revealed that a few managers at NYNEX Material Enterprises Company (MECO) had breached generally accepted principles of business behavior. These managers were either fired from NYNEX or reassigned due to these allegations. Investigating the relationship between MECO and the other NYNEX companies, regulatory commissions in both New York and Massachusetts reaffirmed that an organization such as MECO was important for the economic benefit of the telephone companies.

Recognizing that a company such as MECO should not even have the appearance of any potential conflicts of interest, however, NYNEX initiated and undertook a restructuring of its businesses. The first step in this restructuring was the merging of MECO with the NYNEX Services Company into a company called Telesector Resources Group. Telesector provides the centralized information services, market and regulatory planning functions, and purchasing for both telephone companies.

As a final step in its restructuring, NYNEX's companies

were divided into two groups. The Telecommunications group consisted of New England Telephone, New York Telephone and Telesector Resources Group. The Worldwide Services Group included the operating units of NYNEX Mobile Communications, all of its software and consulting businesses, and NYNEX Network Systems Company.

In the United Kingdom, NYNEX Network Systems and its cable television partners were awarded eleven cable TV franchises. Continuing its entry into the financial services arena, NYNEX acquired Stockholder Systems of Norcross, Georgia and enhanced its standing as the leading U.S. provider of financial applications software.

At NYNEX Mobile a growth rate of better than 20 percent kept the company the leading provider of cellular service in the Northeast. By the end of 1990 NYNEX Mobile served in excess of one quarter million customers. At the wireline networks the percent of digital access lines grew to over 50 percent and nearly 500,000 miles of fiber optic cable were in place.

1991

The recession that had hurt NYNEX's results in 1990 grew worse in 1991. For the first time the company's revenues declined from the previous year, by over $300 million, and a similar decrease in net income occurred.

During the year NYNEX continued to slash expenses and the number of employees decreased from 94,000 to 84,000. The largest source of the decrease was from an early retirement agreement reached with the labor unions in September. Under these agreements approximately 7,300 non-management employees retired during the year. Also, the company ensured the avoidance of any work disruptions in 1992 by signing a new labor agreement in 1991, well in advance of the mid-1992 contract expiration date.

Organizationally, NYNEX further restructured itself during the year. Several businesses were dropped that were not in line with the company's overall mission of helping people communicate through wireline and wireless networks, data-base management, delivery services and information services. To this end, NYNEX exited the real estate development business and sold the NYNEX Business Centers. At the same time, NYNEX Information Resources, publisher of the NYNEX Yellow Pages directories, was transferred to the Worldwide Services Group where NYNEX's non-regulated companies are aligned.

NYNEX Mobile Communications continued its impressive growth rate with 48,500 new customers added during the year, an increase of almost 19 percent, to total over 300,000 customers by the end of the year. In Japan NYNEX began participating in two cellular partnerships to begin operations in 1994. At NYNEX Information Resources the company produced over 32 million directories and began looking into the potential of compact disc based Yellow Pages.

While the number of customer access lines at the NYNEX telephone companies was up a relatively modest 140,000, the companies continued to grow their networks. During the year an additional 164,000 miles of fiber optic cable was laid and the percent of digital access lines grew to 60 percent. The introduction of new services such as RediServ also helped the business grow; RediServ allows for the rapid installation of telephone service to new residence customers by maintaining a connection between the residence and the local switching office after the previous customer disconnects service.

1992

NYNEX began to regain its momentum in 1992. Net income shot up to $1.3 billion, more than double the previous year's $600 million. On a per share basis this amounted to $6.40 compared to $2.98 in 1991.

At NYNEX Mobile Communications over 80,000 additional cellular customers were gained, raising the number served to nearly 400,000. To better serve these customers an additional 127 local transmitters were brought on-line.

Operating income climbed to over $61 million, up more than 25 percent from the previous year.

New York Telephone and New England Telephone continued to move toward the twin goals of providing both a fully digital and fiber-optic based network designed to meet their customers' future needs. By the end of the year two-thirds of NYNEX's nearly 16 million network access lines were being served by digital switches, and 800,000 miles of fiber-optic cable covered the region from Maine to New York City.

NYNEX also continued to take advantage of international expansion opportunities, with a particular focus on the Asia Pacific region. Telephone companies in developing regions such as Micronesia relied on software from the NYNEX DPI Company to automate activities such as customer service, billing and accounting. NYNEX also began participation in a project to construct and operate a two million line telephone network in Bangkok.

NYNEX Information Resources Company (NIRC) continued as the premier provider of Yellow Pages directories in the Northeastern United States. NIRC's Czech subsidiary signed a 13-year contract to publish seven Yellow Pages and white pages directories in the Czech Republic. The company also published its second telephone directory in Gibraltar.

Meeting customers' ever-growing needs requires an investment in research and development, and over $130 million was invested in R&D during the year. The 300 scientists and engineers at NYNEX Science and Technology won five U.S. patents for new technologies to improve cost efficiencies and meet customer needs.

As NYNEX headed toward the end of its first decade of service as a stand-alone corporation, chairman and CEO William C. Ferguson said, "We are enhancing the creativity and drive of NYNEX people around the world to fulfill our corporate mission of helping people communicate—whenever, however and wherever they want."

14

Pacific Telesis

Pacific Bell and Nevada Bell operations were combined at divestiture to create the Pacific Telesis Group. Geographically Pacific Telesis is the smallest of the Bell Holding Companies with all of its telephone and Yellow Pages operations being in the two state region of California and Nevada. The word Telesis is defined as "Progress, Intelligently Planned."

1984

In its first year of operations Pacific Telesis earned almost $830 million on revenues of $7.8 billion. Actual earnings per share were $8.46, well exceeding the company's projection of $8.00 per share. Contributing to the first year's results were tight cost controls which resulted in expenses being 5.7 percent under expectations. As a consequence of these financial results Pacific Telesis stockholders enjoyed a healthy $5.40 per share dividend.

During this first year, Pacific Telesis crafted strategies for deploying and marketing technology, and diversifying into new lines of business. These strategies targeted opportunities where the skills and experience of Pacific Telesis provided a competitive advantage. At the heart of all decisions at Pacific Telesis is the central imperative to continually increase the value of stockholders' investments. To put those words into action the company decided that starting in 1985 as much as 20 percent of the salaries of 23,000 Pacific Telesis managers would depend on the financial performance of the company.

At divestiture, Pacific Bell operated as the telecommunications provider for over 20 million people in California while throughout Nevada 300,000 people lived in Nevada Bell's service area. Pacific Bell, the company's largest subsidiary, employed almost 75,000 people while Nevada Bell customers were served by 1,100 employees. Combined, Pacific Bell and Nevada Bell were serving over 11.3 million access lines at the end of 1984.

Pacific Bell Directory, an independent division of Pacific Bell, published the white pages and Yellow Pages directories for all Pacific Bell and Nevada Bell regional service areas. During 1984, revenues from directory services climbed over 20 percent. Another Pacific Telesis company, PacTel Publishing, was formed to develop and publish specialized regional, national and international directories for consumer and business markets. During 1984, PacTel Publishing entered into agreements to publish specialized directories for the American Hotel and Motel Association, the American Institute of Architects and the American Society of Interior Designers.

Pacific Telesis formed two companies in 1984 to fully take advantage of the potential cellular marketplace. PacTel Mobile Services marketed cellular mobile telephone equipment and resold cellular services in markets such as Dallas, Houston and New York. Meanwhile, PacTel Mobile Access built and operated cellular networks and offered their first service in Los Angeles in June 1984; by the end of that year more than 15,000 customers were being served in the greater Los Angeles area.

1985

In 1985 the Pacific Telesis Group delivered mightily to the company's stockholders. During the year the corporation's revenues increased from $7.8 billion in 1984 to $8.5 billion. This allowed net income to increase by $100 million from 1984's $829 million. On a per share basis earnings were up 7.3 percent to $9.08 and quarterly dividends increased from $1.35 to $1.43, or $5.72 for the year.

The company was well aware that the telephone operations in California and Nevada formed the foundation of Pacific Telesis. Over $2 billion was invested during the year in the core telephone businesses to expand the power and versatility of the network. In 1985, the number of customer lines able to take advantage of equal access went from two percent to over 45 percent. The number of access lines in service grew by 400,000 to reach 11.7 million.

For the PacTel companies 1985 was also an exciting year. At the cellular operations—PacTel Mobile Access—service was introduced in three additional markets: Oxnard/Ventura, San Diego and Sacramento. By the end of 1985 the number of cellular customers had more than tripled to over 51,000. To make sure the quality of the equipment matched the quality of the cellular service provided, PacTel Mobile Services continued to work closely with suppliers to meet customer service objectives.

The new, diversified business requirements of Pacific Telesis also generated needs for new services. Requirements for real estate and financing services resulted in the creation of PacTel Properties and PacTel Finance. PacTel Properties provided property acquisition, development and brokerage services to other Pacific Telesis companies as well as to other business customers. PacTel Financing provided financial support to strengthen the marketing efforts of Pacific Telesis Communications and the cellular companies as their needs grew.

1986

During 1986 the value of Pacific Telesis continued to grow dramatically. Net income reached $1.08 billion, a whopping 16 percent increase over the $929 million reported in 1985. Revenues for the year were up 5.6 percent to nearly $9 billion. At the same time cost controls kept expense increases to only 3.9 percent.

Wall Street continued to regard the company highly and the price of its stock continued to soar. In March, the directors of Pacific Telesis declared a two-for-one stock split. Through the first three years after divestiture, while the Standard & Poor's 500 stock index grew by 51 percent, the value of a share of Pacific Telesis had risen 92 percent by the end of 1986.

In August, Pacific Bell and Nevada Bell signed a new contract with the Communications Workers of America. In this contract an unprecedented employment security agreement offered employees the chance to upgrade their skills through retraining and to be reassigned when new opportunities became available. Another provision in the contract gave employees a personal stake in the business, with part of their annual compensation being based on the companies' successfully achieving certain service and financial objectives.

In 1986, Pacific Bell Directory published advertising for more than 300,000 local businesses. These advertisements appeared in the 28 million copies of 96 different white pages and Yellow Pages directories produced and distributed by the company. Product innovation during the year resulted in the SMART™ Yellow Pages. This new format, included in 1,897 directories, permitted customers to take advantage of new and simplified referencing and other improvements in the content and design of the new directories.

Following a strategy of growth through regional expansion and acquisitions, Pacific Telesis moved forward in 1986 to become one of the largest providers of cellular and paging services in the country. Cellular and paging companies were consolidated under the PacTel Personal Communications Company. In December, PacTel Cellular signed an agreement to acquire Communications Industries Inc., a provider of paging and cellular services, at a cost of over $315 million. Included were cellular operations in the Michigan areas of Detroit, Flint, Grand Rapids, and Lansing as well as in Toledo, Ohio.

1987

At the close of 1987 Pacific Telesis voluntarily took a one time expense charge of $217 million. This resulted from a decision to provide management employees the opportunity to take an enhanced early retirement offer. Nearly 3,000 managers took advantage of the offer. However, beginning in 1988 Pacific Telesis would enjoy an annual savings of between $130 million and $170 million as a result of these early retirements. These savings will continue to flow to the company's bottom line for years into the future.

Omitting the impact of the one-time retirement charge Pacific Telesis had another excellent year. Net income excluding the charge was up 7.6 percent to over $1.13 billion from 1985's $1.05 billion. As in 1986 the company's Board of Directors once again decided to issue a stock dividend. On March 25 another two-for-one stock split was awarded to the stockholders of Pacific Telesis.

During 1987 the number of network access lines in service increased by 450,000 to over 12.5 million. The Pacific Bell and Nevada Bell companies also continued to focus on bringing information to the right places at the right time. A good example of this is voice mail. In 1987 the Federal Communications Commission gave Pacific Bell and Nevada Bell permission to offer this service. While awaiting a waiver from the federal court to provide the service to customers the companies began offering it to employees. Almost 15,000 employees signed up for this service during the trial and regularly enjoy as well as bear testimony to its benefits.

During 1987, PacTel Personal Communications completed the acquisition of the five-region Detroit cellular system and initiated purchases of adjacent properties. In February the cellular system in Atlanta, wholly owned by PacTel, was also brought on-line. These developments and the tremendous growth of the Los Angeles market fueled the impressive growth of cellular. By the end of 1987 PacTel Personal Communications served over 168,000 cellular customers, up from 94,500 at the end of 1986.

Pacific Telesis International focused on sustainable business opportunities during the year, including a digital paging operation in Bangkok. That venture exceeded projections with 17,500 customers signing on in the first year. Pacific

Telesis International also partnered with KICC, a Korean company, to create an information age network linking banks and retail organizations in Korea's first credit card verification system.

1988

A change in leadership was perhaps the most dramatic event at Pacific Telesis in 1988 as Donald E. Guinn, the corporation's first chairman and chief executive officer, took early retirement. Named to replace him in both capacities was Sam Ginn, who had been serving as president and chief operating officer and was the architect of the company's diversification strategy. The retirement of Mr. Guinn, who remained an active member of the company's Board of Directors, signaled the marketplace that Pacific Telesis was accelerating its pace of change.

Pacific Telesis also achieved excellent, record-setting financial results in 1988. Revenues grew to almost $9.5 billion from nearly $9.2 billion the year before. Net income set a record at nearly $1.2 billion and earnings per share were also at a record level of $2.81. Contributing to these figures were the greatly increasing productivity levels at the Pacific Telesis companies. At Pacific Bell and Nevada Bell the average number of access lines served per employee continued its steady climb, ending the year at 198, up 32 percent from 1984. The financial markets continued to reward the company's progress; $1,000 invested in Pacific Telesis stock the day it began trading—November 21, 1983—had grown to be worth nearly $3,000 by the end of 1988.

Explosive customer growth also continued at the Pacific Telesis companies, with Pacific Bell enjoying a record growth of over 550,000 access lines. By the end of the year the number of access lines in service at Pacific Bell and Nevada Bell totaled nearly 13 million. PacTel Cellular's customer base experienced a nearly 60 percent growth with over 262,000 customers on the cellular network by the end of the year.

Other Pacific Telesis companies also continued to

grow. At Pacific Bell Directory several educational and self-help resources for small businesses were developed. Working with the U.S. Small Business Administration new publications such as *Small Business Success* were made available around the country. PacTel Business Systems acquired both ABI American Businessphones and Comprehensive Communications during the year. PacTel Business Systems, which serves customers with two to 250 telephones per office, gained 14,000 installed systems and doubled the size of its business with these acquisitions.

1989

On October 17, 1989, Pacific Bell's network passed an important test when a major earthquake struck northern California. Thanks to lessons learned from previous earthquakes and skills sharpened through emergency drills, the network performed exactly as planned to provide the customers of Pacific Bell service when they needed it most.

Pacific Telesis also achieved its best year ever in terms of financial performance. Net income rose 4.5 percent to $1.24 billion, or $3.02 a share, a 7.5 percent increase over 1988. Revenues reached $9.59 billion, 1.2 percent higher than 1988. All of the company's financial ratios were also in excellent shape. For example, return on equity stood at a record 15.4 percent while the company's profit margin continued its upward trend and rose to 13 percent.

Pacific Bell saw its customer access lines increase by 558,000 during 1989. On the regulatory front the California Public Utilities Commission approved a new regulatory framework calling for nearly $400 million in rate reductions in 1990. However, beginning in 1991 Pacific Telesis would be able to begin reaping the benefits of new, profitable technology at the core telephone operations.

PacTel Cellular continued to set new records during 1989. The customer base grew by 119,000 to 381,000 customers by year's end. Spurred by this growth plus the addition of new cellular services and products, PacTel Cellular's 1989 net income rose 255 percent over 1988, to $55.4 million on revenues of over $450 million. At Pacific Bell Directory, strong customer demand pushed revenues up 9.9 percent to $867 million.

In December, as part of a consortium, Pacific Telesis became the first U.S. telecommunications company to enter the West German market for cellular service. Pacific Telesis held a 26 percent interest in a system that will eventually reach 61 million people. With the reunification of Germany this market would expand to 77 million people. Along with its partners in Great Britain the company was awarded licenses to eventually provide cable television service to 822,000 homes in the United Kingdom. And in Japan, as a member of another partnership venture, Pacific Telesis was the first of the BHCs to enter the international long-distance market between Japan and other countries.

1990

In 1990 Pacific Bell declared its goal to be the customers' choice in the increasingly competitive telecommunications marketplace. To achieve this vision, the company adopted a new organizational structure to help its 60,000 employees deliver quality products and superior customer service.

The strategy for success combined Pacific Bell's ability to provide quality products and services to diverse market segments with the customer focus of a smaller, more entrepreneurial business. The new structure would serve customers through market-focused business units that respond quickly to evolving customer needs. Eight new regional businesses were established, with each unit being responsible for engineering, sales, installation and repair. These regional markets were geographically defined as Los Angeles, the San Francisco Bay Area, Orange County/Riverside, Valley/Central Coast, San Diego/Imperial County, North Coast, and the Hispanic and Asian Markets, which cross all geographic boundaries.

Beyond these markets six additional business units were formed to serve customers and markets that require a statewide focus. These statewide markets were defined as: the Public Sector Market, which included schools, universities and government agencies; National Accounts, servicing large commercial customers with nationwide telecommunications requirements; the Industry Market, which included companies that sell telecommunications or information services; Public Communications, which was assigned pay-phone market responsibilities; Operator Services, which provided call completion and directory assistance services; and finally, Information Services, which was assigned responsibility for certain enhanced telecommunications services such as voice mail and electronic messaging.

The anticipated $400 million rate reduction for 1990 turned out to be about $500 million. However, it was anticipated that the new regulatory framework would prove to be in the long-term interest of Pacific Telesis and its customers. Also, during the year Pacific Telesis decided it was not a real estate company and started to sell off its PacTel Properties portfolio. The sell-off caused the company to book a $60 million reduction and a 1.2 percent decrease in net income. For the year, however, Pacific Telesis still earned $1.03 billion on revenues of $9.71 billion.

1991

While California maintained its position as one of the world's strongest growth markets there is no question the recession of 1991 adversely impacted the results of Pacific Telesis. For the year net income was virtually unchanged at $1.02 billion. Chairman and CEO Sam Ginn said of 1991, "Overall, given the state of the economy, I believe we had a respectable year, not an outstanding one."

Pacific Telesis continued to build for the future by investing capital to meet the needs of its customers. All told, $2.2 billion was invested during the year in maintaining the network and deploying upgrades. New technology such as Signaling System 7 (SS7) was being deployed in San Francisco and Los Angeles in 1991. SS7 technology provided additional new features such as Call Return and Caller ID to both residential and business customers. It also provided Pacific Bell's largest customers, the inter-exchange carriers, with more sophisticated interconnections.

With the telephone companies continuing to generate the largest share of Pacific Telesis revenues, the regulatory front remained of paramount importance. During 1991 Nevada Bell began operating under a more flexible regulatory plan. This new incentive-based framework placed a five-year cap on basic rates and also allowed shareowners and customers to share in Nevada Bell's profits. Pacific Bell submitted proposals to the California Public Utilities Commission to establish rates that responded to competitive threats and reflected the true costs of providing individual services.

In August 1991 PacTel and McCaw Cellular announced plans to combine their cellular systems in Dallas, Kansas City, San Francisco and San Jose in a joint venture as equal partners. With the completion of this transaction in 1992 PacTel Cellular would have a significant presence in nine of the country's top 25 cellular markets: Atlanta, Cincinnati, Cleveland, Dallas, Detroit, Kansas City, Los Angeles, San Diego and San Francisco. PacTel also purchased McCaw's properties in Wichita and Topeka, Kansas. By the end of 1991 PacTel Cellular was serving 550,000 customers nationwide, 32 percent more than at the end of 1990. With the signing of the McCaw agreements the future prospects for PacTel's Cellular growth were indeed promising.

1992

Pacific Telesis stunned the industry when it announced its decision to spin-off its wireless operations into an entirely independent corporation. This decision was made following an exhaustive eight-month analysis. The conclusions were that if the wireless operations were to take advantage of the industry's revolution they needed more freedom—chiefly financial and regulatory—in their actions. It was anticipated the spin-off would be completed by early 1994.

The wireline company would be called Pacific Telesis and would be headed by Philip J. Quigley as chairman and CEO. After the spin-off it would continue to own local telephone operations in California and Nevada as well as the directory publishing business. Investors would be targeted who want to buy stock in a company noted for its stability and dividend producing ability.

The wireless company, nameless as of now, would be headed by Sam Ginn as chairman and CEO. The principle components would be the PacTel cellular and paging functions as well as all international operations. This company would not pay dividends but would reinvest all available cash in building the business, thereby attracting growth-oriented investors.

A review of the financial performance of both companies supports this decision. The "new" Pacific Telesis would have maintained annual revenues of about $8.7 billion and earnings of $1 billion if it had been a separate entity between 1990 and 1992. On the other hand the new wireless company would have experienced sharp increases in revenue from about $600 million in 1990 to nearly $900 million in 1992, while in the same period net income would have gone down from $60 million to $20 million.

As work toward the spin-off continued Sam Ginn said, "In the meantime, let me assure you that we will continue to work as one company, maintaining the fabric of this organization and focusing on our number one job—to serve our customers well and provide value for our shareowners."

15

Southwestern Bell

Southwestern Bell Corporation was the only Bell Holding Company whose telephone and Yellow Pages operations remained the same before and after divestiture. Southwestern Bell's telephone and publishing operations include the states of Arkansas, Kansas, Missouri, Oklahoma and Texas.

1984

In its first post-divestiture year Southwestern Bell posted net income of $883 million on revenues of $7.2 billion. Expressed on a per share basis earnings were $9.04 while the annual dividend amounted to $5.60 per share.

By the end of 1984, Southwestern Bell was composed of four primary operating subsidiaries: Southwestern Bell Telephone, which managed the telephone operations in all five states it served; Southwestern Bell Mobile Systems, the cellular phone component; Southwestern Bell Publications, the Yellow Pages publishing arm; and Southwestern Bell Telecom, which provided telecommunications equipment for consumers and businesses.

Southwestern Bell's telephone operations served over 10.6 million customer access lines in 1984. Its network contained 16,000 miles of fiber optic cable and over 70 percent of customers were being served from electronic switching systems, the highest percentage of electronic switching of the divested companies. These systems provide customers the ability to have their voice and data transmitted quickly and efficiently, and make available many enhanced services.

Recognizing the importance of customer service, the Rider Service Award was established at the telephone company to recognize employees who go beyond the call of duty in providing outstanding customer service. The award was named after Charles E. Rider, the only Southwestern Bell employee to earn a gold Vail award. Rider earned this award in 1923 for his heroic efforts in protecting toll lines in the aftermath of a fiery train wreck. He was so proud of the medal that he had it imbedded in his tombstone when he died of cancer only five months after receiving the award.

Southwestern Bell Mobile Systems aggressively entered the cellular marketplace in 1984. By the end of the year cellular systems were up and running in Dallas/Fort Worth, Kansas City and St. Louis. Mobile Systems also became a reseller of other cellular providers' services; in markets from Los Angeles to Phoenix to Miami, Mobile Systems began to tap into the future of cellular communications.

Southwestern Bell Publications produced more than 35 million copies of 464 Yellow Pages and white pages directories during the year. Southwestern Bell Publications also introduced an innovative new product called Silver Pages. This was the company's first nationwide product, listing agencies and businesses offering special services and discounts to senior citizens.

Southwestern Bell Telecom began the year without any customers, but by the end of 1984 it had sold more than 11,000 business telecommunications systems in 20 states and sales had exceeded $100 million. Telecom also acquired the Indianapolis-based Freedom Phone Division of Electra Company. This division served the small business and consumer markets for cordless telephones and was later expanded to include corded and cellular telephones.

1985

Nineteen eighty-five was a year of double digit growth for Southwestern Bell. For the year revenues rose 10.2 percent to over $7.9 billion and net income was up 12.8 percent to slightly under $1 billion. Earnings per share also climbed more than 10.5 percent to an even $10.00 and shareholders were rewarded with an annual dividend of $6.00 per share, a seven percent increase over 1984.

During 1985 access line growth at Southwestern Bell Telephone was up 300,000 lines to close the year at 10.9 million lines in service. Electronic switching was available to three quarters of these lines by the end of the year. And, 2.7 million of these lines benefitted by taking advantage of this technology's Custom Calling features. Features such as Call Waiting and Three Way Calling delivered valuable service to customers and additional revenues to the company.

Southwestern Bell Publications expanded both its geographic service area and its product lines in 1985, with key acquisitions fueling this expansion. Mast Advertising and Publishing was acquired from Continental Telecom. This acquisition gave the company a position in national Yellow Pages sales and in directory sales for independent telephone companies. New York Yellow Pages was acquired to give the company a presence in the competitive New York City market area.

By the end of 1985 Southwestern Bell Mobile Systems was providing service to some 35,000 customers and had processed over 100 million calls during the year. Cellular systems were operating in St. Louis, Kansas City, Dallas/Ft. Worth, Oklahoma City, San Antonio and Wichita. In total over $50 million in capital expenditures had resulted in a total market coverage of some 14,000 square miles, an increase of nearly 230 percent over 1984.

While once again surpassing $100 million in sales, Southwestern Bell Telecom re-examined the manner in which it served the telecommunications marketplace. As a result of this review the company decided to split the marketing and customer service functions into separate groups. This allowed an increased focus on its customer service responsibilities while increasing the financial focus through each group operating as an independent profit center.

1986

In 1986 Southwestern Bell saw its revenues drop by about $23 million to slightly over $7.9 billion, or a decrease of 0.3 percent. Most of this drop was attributable to telephone company refunds on interstate access revenues. Despite this revenue reduction the company still posted an increase in net income of 2.7 percent due to stringent cost controls. For the year net income was $10.26 a share as opposed to $10.00 the previous year, and dividends rose to $6.40 from $6.00 a share.

Southwestern Bell's charter declared the corporation to be "a quality communications company serving the needs of the information marketplace while pursuing selective expansion opportunities that capitalize on the strength of its resources." Universally available, high-quality telephone service remained a basic component of that charter.

With respect to evaluating expansion opportunities Southwestern Bell established three criteria. Acceptable opportunities must increase the value of shareholder investment, build on corporate strengths and areas of expertise, and enhance the corporation's position as a quality communications company.

During 1986 Southwestern Bell took two major steps consistent with this strategy. Plans were unveiled at Southwestern Bell Publications to publish Yellow Pages directories in four major markets outside its traditional five state area. Those markets were New York City, Baltimore, Chicago and Washington, D.C.

Meanwhile, the stage was set to enlarge the corporation's cellular operations in 1987 should a planned acquisition of industry leader Metromedia, Inc. be approved by the courts. The Metromedia acquisition would also make Southwestern Bell one of the nation's largest providers of paging services.

In June of 1986 Southwestern Bell significantly altered the management structure between the corporation and the telephone company. Zane E. Barnes, who had been serving as the president and chief executive officer of both the corporation and the telephone company, relinquished the telephone company positions to John E. Hayes, Jr. Mr. Barnes retained the corporation titles and also remained the corporation's chairman.

1987

On September 30, 1987, Southwestern Bell legally wagered $1.4 billion on the future of the cellular and paging industries. The acquisition of Metromedia passed all legal roadblocks and was put into effect. For the $1.4 billion Southwestern Bell acquired six Cellular One properties. Four of the six were in the top 15 U.S markets, including Chicago, Boston, Washington, D.C. and Baltimore. These properties retained the well-established Cellular One name but were organized under Southwestern Bell Mobile Systems. By the end of 1987 Mobile Systems was efficiently serving 155,000 customers in 21 markets throughout the United States.

The new paging company, Metromedia Paging Services, was organized as a separate, wholly-owned subsidiary, with over 600,000 paging customers being served in 30 markets across the United States.

Another acquisition during the year was that of Gulf Printing company. Gulf Printing was a publisher of directories as well as one of the largest commercial printers in the U.S. This acquisition provided vertical integration of SBC's directory publishing business by adding production capabilities to the existing components of product development, sales and marketing.

Despite a sluggish economy in Southwestern Bell Telephone's geographic territory the company continued to build for the future. Access line growth by the end of 1987 was up only 22,000 over 1986 to stand at 11.1 million lines. The company still invested over $1.4 billion during the year to maintain and upgrade the network, and electronic switching increased from 83 percent of access lines served to 87 percent.

Putting something back into the communities it serves is the function of the Southwestern Bell Foundation. During the year the Foundation made grants totaling nearly $12 million to a variety of social, cultural and educational needs. The Foundation underwrote a tour of works by artist Georgia O'Keeffe to mark the centennial of her birth. Some 120 pieces of her art were displayed in Washington, D.C., Chicago, Dallas and New York.

1988

In October of 1988 Southwestern Bell Corporation signaled a generational change in leadership when Edward E. Whitacre, Jr. was named president and chief operating officer of the corporation. It was also announced that at the end of 1989 he would become chairman and chief executive officer. In so doing he replaced the company's first chairman, Zane E. Barnes. At age 47 Mr. Whitacre was twenty years younger than the venerable Mr. Barnes.

Changes in 1988 were not limited to the company's management. The Silver Pages specialty directories and the company's Yellow Pages operations in New York, Chicago and Pinalles County, Florida were not meeting expectations for a variety of reasons. Feeling it had enough information to make some tough decisions, Southwestern Bell decided to terminate these operations and write-off the losses.

Despite the costs of these write-offs and the increased interest expense associated with the Metromedia purchase the company saw a modest increase in net income of 1.2 percent, to $1.06 billion. More encouraging was a 5.6 percent increase in revenues to over $8.45 billion.

Southwestern Bell Telephone's access line growth picked up sharply over 1987's anemic increases. At the end of 1988 the company was serving over 11.3 million access lines, an increase of 235,000 from the year before. The number of employees per 10,000 access lines had dropped from 67.1 at divestiture to 51.1 for a 23 percent increase in efficiency.

Growth continued unabated at Southwestern Bell Mobile Systems in 1988. The customer base climbed to 244,000 as contrasted to 155,000 at the end of 1987, a growth rate of nearly 60 percent. With the addition of the McAllen,

Brownsville and Abilene markets, all in Texas, the company was now providing cellular service in 24 markets throughout the United States.

Southwestern Bell also expanded its presence in the international marketplace. The company had made the world aware of its interest in the international arena through its limited Yellow Pages activities in Israel and Australia. In 1988 Southwestern Bell Telecom began to market its Freedom Phone line in the United Kingdom, and also introduced the U.K.'s first private pay phones for businesses.

1989

Nineteen eighty-nine saw Southwestern Bell post record levels of achievement in revenues and net income. Revenues for the year were over $8.7 billion with net income at $1.1 billion, both figures representing gains of over three percent from the results of 1988. This year also saw Edward Whitacre elevated to chairman and CEO as Zane Barnes retired.

At Southwestern Bell Telephone the introduction of new services and a stronger regional economy provided a healthy base for improved results. During 1989 the number of access lines in service increased by nearly 420,000. New SS7 Call Control Options such as Call Blocking, Selective Call Forwarding and the ability to redial the last incoming call were brought on-line in the telephone company's region during the year. The offering of these services to new and existing customers provided a new source of revenues with tremendous possibilities.

The telephone company also continued to strive for regulatory change that would allow improved customer service and ensure healthy earnings. In Kansas, Missouri and Texas the regulatory commissions either approved or were considering plans that called for changing traditional rate-of-return regulation. These changes included major network improvements which allowed both the company and its customers to enjoy the benefits of improved operations.

Following a major restructuring in 1988, Southwestern Bell Publications continued to seek out new opportunities in 1989. In four markets the company trialed the innovative Mobile Yellow Pages, which gave car phone users a compact version of the regular Yellow Pages directory designed to fit in a car's glove compartment.

The 1987 acquisition of Metromedia Paging and Cellular One continued to prove a positive strategic move. Growth at the Cellular One properties and in the Mobile Systems markets resulted in an increase of almost 140,000 customers during the year. By the end of the year 382,000 customers in 24 markets relied on Southwestern Bell for their cellular service. At Metromedia Paging nearly 810,000 pagers were being served in 32 markets, with both local and regional coverage.

Under new F.C.C. regulations Southwestern Bell's Telecom and telephone operations were allowed to begin team-selling products and services during 1989. This allowed business customers a much-desired single point-of-contact to fulfill their telecommunications requirements. Telecom's Freedom Phone Division saw its consumer and small business products being offered by retailers in all 50 states, the United Kingdom, Canada and New Zealand.

1990

On December 20, 1990, a consortium consisting of Southwestern Bell, France Telecom and Grupo Carso of Mexico acquired 51 percent of the full-voting common stock of Telefonos de Mexico, or Telmex. Southwestern Bell's share of the $1.76 billion purchase price was $485 million. For this, Southwestern Bell acquired 12.5 percent of the full-voting common shares, five percent of the equity, and an option to purchase an additional five percent of the equity in the richly promising Mexican telephone company.

In one bold move Southwestern Bell became a major partner in Telmex. Telmex is the exclusive provider of local telephone service and both national and international long-distance in Mexico. Telmex also provides other services such as cellular, paging and directory advertising.

The consortium's stated objective was to invest heavily in the modernization and expansion of the Mexican telephone system. At the time of the acquisition Telmex was well known for the poor level of service it provided and the rich opportunities for improvement. With a strong commitment to improving service Southwestern Bell and its partners were confident they would be able to rapidly grow the Telmex business.

During 1990 Southwestern Bell's telephone operations continued to build the customer base. Nearly 350,000 new access lines were added to the network so that by the end of the year the number of lines served had climbed to over 12 million. In continuing to build for the future the company also added over 100,000 miles of fiber optic cable, bringing the total to more than 370,000 miles in service.

Southwestern Bell's publications group saw its revenues grow 8.5 percent to over $794 million. The commitment of employees to satisfy customers resulted in over 96 percent of those customers rating the service they received as good or excellent. Fully 75 percent marked their customer service as excellent.

The company's other operations also grew during the year. The cellular company added 285,000 customers to end the year with 667,000 customers on-line. Nearly 65,000 new paging customers were added to bring that total to 874,000. Revenues from Telecom's Business Systems division grew nearly 25 percent. In Israel the cable television operation had attained a subscription rate of 20 percent of potential households after only one year of operation.

1991

In 1991 Southwestern Bell made two moves that resulted in a decrease in net income from the 1990 level. The company decided to refinance three quarters of a billion dollars in debt to take advantage of lower interest rates. The company also offered most of its 16,000 management employees an early retirement incentive that was accepted by 3,700 managers.

These two steps cost the company $110 million in 1991, but beginning in 1992 the savings from these two measures would outweigh the cost every year from then on.

For the year revenues grew $220 million to $9.33 billion while net income was down by $25 million to nearly $1.08 billion. On a per share basis this translated to net income of $3.58 and a dividend of $2.84. At the end of 1991 the company's stock price was over $64 a share, up more than 15 percent from the same time in 1990.

During the year the company also exercised its option to purchase an additional five percent of Telmex. This brought the company's total investment in Telmex to $953 million. By the end of 1991 the market value of these shares had climbed to $2.5 billion and Wall Street heralded the wisdom of the purchase. Southwestern Bell was not merely an idle investor, but had also established a team of employees based in Mexico City. These managers were developing action plans to improve Telmex's network maintenance, office procedures, billing, cellular service and Yellow Pages.

Growth statistics continued to come in from across the Southwestern Bell family of companies. Southwestern Bell Telephone saw its customer base grow as 293,000 access lines were added. At Telmex over 670,000 access lines were added to the network during the year. Southwestern Bell's cellular operations also saw a gain identical to the telephone company of 293,000 customers, and closed the year with 960,000 customers.

Southwestern Bell also fulfilled its obligation to share corporate resources and talent in the communities it serves. Projects such as Yellow Pages' ReDirectory, a directory recycling program, help the environment and the quality of life in many of the cities the company serves. The company also continued to underwrite research efforts aimed at determining how the education system can be improved.

1992

Southwestern Bell's total return—stock appreciation and dividends—to its shareowners was up 19 percent for the year as the company remained focused on meeting customer needs. Revenues passed the $10 billion level for the first time, up over seven percent from 1991, while net income was up 21 percent to set a record at $1.3 billion.

The company's core telephone operations were reorganized into three smaller companies, each with its own president, reporting to the corporation's CEO. Southwestern Bell Telephone Company of the Midwest, headed by J. Cliff Eason, focuses on serving customers in Missouri, Oklahoma, Kansas and Arkansas. Southwestern Bell Telephone Company of Texas, headed by William E. Dryer, serves customers in Texas. Southwestern Bell Services, headed by Royce S. Caldwell, was established to meet the other two companies' centralized needs. This action was taken with the goal of being able to more quickly meet the changing requirements of the marketplace.

The company also shocked the industry when it announced that it would move the corporation's headquarters from St. Louis to San Antonio. This move was motivated by the fact that more than half the company's business already comes from Texas, and most future growth will take place in Texas and in Mexico, its neighbor to the south. Noted management guru Tom Peters called the decision, "a brilliant move" and a paradigm of the dramatic changes other Fortune 500 companies must make to prosper.

In 1993, as the end of the first decade since divestiture approached, chairman and CEO Edward E. Whitacre, Jr. reaffirmed the company's commitment to its customers. "We are working hard to deliver the products and services customers need today," Whitacre said, "as well as the quality and value they expect. The key is to keep focused on the needs of our customers in the businesses we know best."

16

U S WEST

U S WEST was created at divestiture by combining the former AT&T operating companies of Mountain Bell, Northwestern Bell and Pacific Northwest Bell. U S WEST was geographically the largest Bell Holding Company formed with operations in 14 states. Included in this area are the states of Minnesota, Iowa, North and South Dakota, Nebraska, Montana, Wyoming, Colorado, Arizona, New Mexico, Utah, Idaho, Washington and Oregon.

1984

When U S WEST began operations on January 1, 1984, it set a goal to earn $878 million, or $8.96 per share, in net income during its first year of operation. The company surpassed its goal by achieving earnings of $887 million, or $9.24 per share. Contributing to these results is the fact that in 1984 the region served by U S WEST's telephone operations was the fastest growing region in the United States. Also, that growth was taking place in towns and cities including Denver, where the cost of adding new customer lines was low.

During 1984 $1.6 billion was invested to enlarge and modernize the Mountain Bell, Northwestern Bell and Pacific Northwest Bell communications networks. This included aggressive new programs to put high-speed digital systems and fiber optic systems into service in several major cities. However, by approaching growth with caution the company kept actual expenditures to $188 million less than originally planned. A cautious approach ensured meeting the needs of

U S WEST's customers while also fulfilling the needs of its stockholders and employees.

The employees of U S WEST's new subsidiaries proved they can be successful competitors, too. At U S West Direct, created from the directory departments of the three telephone companies, 35 million copies of some 300 telephone directories were published and distributed throughout the 14 state area. U S West Direct was established as a subsidiary of LANDMARK Publishing, which was itself established to pursue other opportunities in the publishing industry.

NewVector Communications was established to offer cellular mobile phone service for U S WEST. Getting off to a fast start, NewVector Communications led the industry by putting four systems into service during its first year. Plus, the systems in those cities—Minneapolis-St. Paul, Denver, Seattle and Phoenix—all exceeded expectations for the number of customers signing up for service during the year.

1985

For the year U S WEST enjoyed a 7.3 percent increase in revenues to $7.8 billion from $7.3 billion in 1984. Net income also increased from $887 million to $926 million, up 4.4 percent. Negatively impacting net income was an agreement reached to settle two antitrust suits previously filed by MCI. These settlements allowed U S WEST to close a chapter that began long before the breakup of the Bell System.

U S WEST responded to the intensely competitive and constantly changing business communications market by creating a new company called U S WEST Information Systems. This company provided a unified sales and service force that had the flexibility to meet customer needs by offering the best of the telephone companies' services along with the best solutions from the other subsidiaries. U S West Information Systems was established to provide business customers reliable, state-of-the-art, compatible products and services.

NewVector Communications experienced tremendous growth during the year. Highlights included the company receiving approval for a joint venture to build a system serving the Gulf of Mexico; completing plans to build a system in Costa Rica; announcing its intention to purchase a cellular system which would serve San Diego, the nation's tenth largest cellular market; and buying part of the cellular system serving Omaha.

LANDMARK, the publishing company, also bought a San Diego firm, Trans Western Publishing. LANDMARK also announced plans to expand by acquiring Lomar/Johnson Directory Publishing Companies. Lomar was one of the largest independent publishers of telephone directories in the country, while Johnson Publishing was the nation's second-largest publisher of city directories.

Doing more with less was the key phrase at U S WEST's telephone companies. By the end of 1985 the telephone companies had increased the number of customer access lines in service by over 610,000 so that the total number in service topped 11.2 million. This was accomplished despite an almost eight percent reduction in its number of employees. Modernization of the network continued with the three telephone companies spending nearly $2 billion to bring new technology to the growing base of customers.

1986

Revenues for the year increased by 6.3 percent to $8.3 billion while net income was off by $2 million to $924 million. A key contributor to this decline was a one-time $52 million write-off associated with a major restructuring of U S West Information Systems, the business communications equipment unit. Essentially, management decided national sales volumes and margins did not justify the continued development of the subsidiary outside of the corporation's traditional 14 state region. This move allowed U S WEST to stop the operating losses it was incurring and instead target other high-growth potential businesses.

By the end of 1986 over 75 percent of the telephone customers served by U S WEST companies were served by computer managed call-switching centers. The deployment of fiber optic cable continued during the year, resulting in over 80 thousand miles being in service by the end of 1986. These and other investments in the network allowed customers to send more information, faster and more accurately.

LANDMARK Publishing continued its expansion as a national company during the year. By moving into new areas and acquiring 11 companies in 1986, LANDMARK had grown to be the publisher of over 850 city and telephone directories in 45 states. It also obtained a printing company and became a provider of marketing-related services for the directory industry.

At U S WEST Cellular the acquisition of the San Diego cellular system was completed. By year's end U S WEST Cellular was providing high-quality cellular service to over 40,000 customers in 13 cities. The company also introduced service in the Gulf of Mexico to meet the communications needs of the offshore oil and fishing industries.

U S WEST Financial Services had become one of the top finance companies in the nation by the end of 1986. Financial services such as equipment leasing and financial sales assistance resulted in over $1 billion being financed for customers. At BetaWest, U S WEST's real estate company, assets totalled over $700 million. The Portfolio at BetaWest included major office buildings and retail buildings throughout the United States.

U S WEST declared its decision to be guided by the following strategies. First, focus on customers to meet their needs in selected markets. Second, serve customers effectively by providing them with exceptional value. Third, seek the right to meet the competition on equal terms. Fourth, keep regulated and unregulated operations separate to ensure that one doesn't subsidize the other. And finally, diversify within the information industry and into areas that support the industry.

1987

U S WEST enjoyed its first billion dollar year in net income during 1987. For the year net income was up almost 9 percent to slightly over $1 billion on revenues of $8.4 billion. On a per share basis this translated to $5.31 in earnings; a dividend increase of almost 8 percent enlarged the payout to $3.28.

During the year the company undertook a major restructuring. Historically, U S WEST had been organized around the products it sold and the places it served, as are most corporations. However, a new organizational structure was put into place in 1987 based on a definition of a market not being a place but being people with similar needs. To underscore this new approach the three U S WEST Bell companies began to market some products and services under the brand name U S WEST Communications. This allowed the companies to establish a common identity while capitalizing on the value of the Bell name and symbol.

During the first four years since divestiture the combined workforce at all U S WEST companies had decreased by only a little over 2,200 employees, to 68,523. However, at the three telephone companies serving the traditional 14-state region the number of employees had decreased by nearly 13,000. Hard-working employees registered tremendous increases in efficiency at the telephone companies which allowed the number of employees to grow by over 10,000 at the other subsidiaries in this four year period.

During 1987 U S WEST Financial Services doubled its portfolio of leases and loans for customers around the world. Gross receivables stood at $2 billion and its percentage of delinquent accounts was among the lowest in the industry. At the commercial real estate company, BetaWest, the value of assets climbed nearly 25 percent to total over $875 million.

At the wireless subsidiaries growth continued to surpass the competition. At the 15 markets served by U S WEST Cellular the average market penetration was 13 percent higher than the industry average. U S WEST Paging enjoyed a 155 percent growth rate, a full 50 percent higher than the industry average for this vital statistic.

Smaller U S WEST companies also enjoyed successes in helping their customers during 1987. For example U S WEST Knowledge Engineering developed software and database products to help manage information. One of their applications software packages helped local governments throughout the arid West manage vital water supplies.

1988

The restructuring that began at U S WEST's telephone operations in 1987 was fully implemented in 1988 with the establishment of the U S WEST Communications Group. U S WEST Communications formally became the new name for all of the telephone operations at Mountain Bell, Northwestern Bell and Pacific Northwest Bell.

This name change was followed with the formation of new market units so that a tight focus was on customers served. Market units were established for home and personal services, large business services, small business services, information providers such as voice mail, government and education services, federal services, the long distance carriers, and the other local telephone companies in U S WEST's region.

The establishment of these market units under a single entity began to chip away at the geographical marketing mindset. The regulatory agencies in each of the 14 states served by U S WEST continue to somewhat force a geographic alignment of operations. However, customers still gain from this alignment due to the focusing of company resources on the diverse needs of the different markets.

Beyond the Communications Group U S WEST had five other principal operating subsidiaries in place five years after divestiture. U S WEST NewVector Group provided paging and cellular services; BetaWest Properties was the full service real estate company; Applied Communications sold software services; U S WEST Financial Services was the diversified financial company; and U S WEST Marketing Resources Group provided telephone and city directories nationwide.

International opportunities began to turn into realities during 1988. In France and throughout the United Kingdom U S WEST International began to enter the cable television marketplace. Holding minority interests of between 10 and 25 percent in several companies provided U S WEST entry into the growing cable television market. Of future interest is the fact that in the United Kingdom cable television franchises carry with them a telecommunications license.

U S West decided to make a public offering of its NewVector Group early in 1988. Less than twenty percent of the stock in NewVector was made available to the public, with U S WEST retaining the other 80 percent. From the offering U S WEST booked an after-tax gain of nearly $90 million. The implication is that a company that came into existence five scant years before was now valued at around $500 million, after-taxes.

1989

Nineteen eighty-nine was an exciting and successful year for U S WEST. Net income totalled over $1.1 billion on revenues of almost $9.7 billion. After backing out the results of the one-time gain in 1988 from the sale of the U S WEST NewVector stock the company's earnings per share grew to $6.02 from $5.69 in 1988. Similarly, dividends per share grew from $3.52 in 1988 to $3.76 for 1989.

In 1989 U S WEST Communications enjoyed its strongest customer-line growth since U S WEST was created. The number of access lines grew by 2.9 percent overall, 3.5 percent for the critically important business lines, and by the end of the year over ten million customers were being served.

Communications products such as Call Waiting and Call Forwarding and second lines for homes and small businesses had strong demand during the year. These gains and others resulted from the market units established in 1988 to serve specific groups of customers. Additionally, U S WEST committed itself to increase the investment in the telephone networks over the next five years by an additional fifteen percent per year.

At U S WEST NewVector the cellular and paging operations enjoyed robust levels of growth. The number of cellular customers served grew by over 60 percent to nearly 135,000. Cellular revenues also enjoyed tremendous growth to nearly $190 million. The number of paging customers being served rose to over 134,000 during the year for a 48 percent increase over 1988.

Cellular growth was not limited to the United States. As a major partner, U S WEST International had become a member of a consortium building a cellular phone system in Hungary, the first in eastern Europe. U S WEST International continued to build the cable television business in Hong Kong, France and the United Kingdom.

In the financial services arena U S WEST Capital Corporation was formed as the holding company for all of U S WEST's financial services. Late in 1989 the Financial Security Assurance company was acquired, increasing the dominance of U S WEST as a financial services company. The role of these financial services also shifted from that of a general leasing and asset-based lending company to specialization in carefully targeted markets.

1990

On December 31, 1991, Jack A. MacAllister retired from his position as the first chief executive officer of U S WEST. Named to replace him was Richard D. McCormick who had been serving as the president of U S WEST. However, Mr. Macallister did retain his position as the chairman of the board of U S WEST.

In the seven years Mr. MacAllister headed U S WEST the company enjoyed tremendous success. Annual revenues grew by 37 percent, to nearly $10 billion; annual net income increased some 35 percent, to $1.2 billion; and assets were up 58 percent, to $27 billion.

On April 19, 1990, U S WEST announced a two-for-one stock split. This was the second such split in six years, the goal being to keep the stock price at an attractive level for individual and institutional investors. For the year the quarterly dividend stood at a split-adjusted $0.50 a share, up 48 percent since divestiture.

U S WEST Marketing Resources Group, home of the directory publishing and marketing services operations, enjoyed a record year in 1990 with a 9.4 percent increase in revenues.

During the year an international operations headquarters was established in Brussels, Belgium, to explore international marketing opportunities. Other international activities saw U S WEST companies launch the first cellular system in eastern Europe when service was turned up in Budapest. Working with Bell Atlantic and other partners plans were also laid out to construct a cellular system in Czechoslovakia. Additional cable television partnerships for franchises in Norway and Sweden were established.

U S WEST NewVector experienced the value of providing excellent customer service as the company continued to grow. For 1990 the number of cellular customers increased over 50 percent to 210,000 while the number of paging customers grew 20 percent to 161,000. At the end of 1990 U S WEST announced plans to buy back the 19 percent interest in NewVector that it had sold to the public in 1988.

1991

By many measures 1991 was a difficult and challenging year financially for U S WEST. While total revenues for the year were up over $600 million net income fell by more than half to $553 million from almost $1.2 billion in 1990. Behind the biggest bulk of this decline was a restructuring charge of $590 million after taxes. The restructuring charge covered the cost of exiting the real estate business, the write-off of intangible assets, and projected costs associated with planned workforce reductions.

The largest portion—the costs associated with exiting the real estate business—had been lurking on the horizon since early 1990. In February of 1990 U S WEST changed its relationship with the real estate subsidiary, BetaWest Properties. U S WEST retained the portfolio of operating properties while a newly formed entity, retaining the BetaWest name, remained active in the field of real estate development.

By early 1991 U S WEST had announced plans to sell all of its real estate portfolio to allow the company to focus on other markets with more predictable returns. At the end of 1990, for example, U S West sold 530,000 square feet of office space in Arizona. Through 1991 the company continued to sell off properties and by the end of the year bit the bullet to absorb the entire cost of exiting the business.

Other U S WEST companies enjoyed favorable results during the year. At U S WEST Communications the three percent growth in the number of telephone access lines was among the highest in the industry. The sales of new products and services such as Voice Messaging, Caller ID and self-healing networks surpassed all initial expectations.

In July of 1991 U S WEST acquired the publicly held portion of U S WEST NewVector to again make it a wholly owned subsidiary. By the end of 1991 the number of cellular and paging customers at NewVector had continued to grow dramatically. The number of cellular customers stood at 293,000, up nearly 40 percent, while paging experienced a 30 percent increase to 210,000 customers.

Internationally, the outlook for the future was equally promising. In a little over a year the Budapest cellular property had signed up 8,000 customers. With Russian partners in St. Petersburg and Moscow the country's first commercial networks were brought into operation. In Great Britain U S WEST entered into a joint venture to share costs in the development of a Personal Communications Network.

1992

As U S WEST emerged from the 1991 restructuring it found itself with a solid performance in 1992. For the year revenues were off due to exiting the real estate business, but still stood at $10.3 billion. Net income for the year would have more than doubled to almost $1.2 billion had the company not taken a non-cash charge of nearly $1.8 billion to cover the future cost of retiree health benefits.

U S WEST continued to build its core telephone operations by investing $2.4 billion to modernize its network. This allowed it to introduce or expand services such as Voice Messaging, Caller ID and Call Trace in 1992. A new service option to be introduced in 1993 is called Stand-By Line and lets small businesses economically manage their communications with an extra line they only need, and pay for, part of the time.

U S WEST NewVector, using the brand names U S WEST Cellular and U S WEST Paging, experienced a tremendous growth in the number of customers being served. The number of cellular customers climbed by 40 percent to total 410,000 while the number of paging customers stood at 247,000, up 18 percent.

Internationally, U S WEST's focus continued in two primary business areas: cable TV/telephone networks and wireless communications. In the United Kingdom its fledgling network was serving 143,000 cable TV customers, up from 88,000 the year before, while 76,000 telephone customers were being served, up from 21,000. In Russia, U S WEST along with its partners continued to develop a digital cellular network. Service was already being provided in Moscow and St. Petersburg, as well as in Hungary, the Czech Republic and Slovakia.

In May, Jack A. MacAllister retired as chairman of U S WEST. CEO Richard D. McCormick was elected by the Board of Directors to replace him. Looking to the future Mr. McCormick said, "The goal that unites all of us is to improve continually the ways we bring people together through communications."

Postscript

Service in the Next Decade

In 1954 Peter Drucker wrote, "There is only one valid definition of business purpose: to create a satisfied customer." In a recent *Telephony* magazine article the consulting firm of McKinsey and Company added, "There's nothing new about the idea of keeping the customer satisfied. What is new in the 1990's is customer satisfaction as the differentiating factor. It is already the case in many industries, and is becoming the case in the local exchange business."

The Most Important Thing You Can Do

The most important consideration involving customer service may be a company's willingness to honestly assess the quality of its service, then provide the focus and resources to move the needle in the right direction. Current service levels are not nearly as important as a commitment to improve; service is rarely too good, and in many cases can be better.

As companies downsize, efforts to provide quality service may be enhanced due to less bureaucracy. Those efforts may also be impeded, however, if cost-cutting measures overemphasize efficiency for efficiency's sake. Increased *effectiveness* should be the goal. The two sound similar, but effectiveness includes the critical variables of employee fulfillment and customer satisfaction.

The Price of Excellence: Eternal Vigilence

"Doing more with less," is the frequent rallying cry of the 1990's. This is terrific so long as it is less fat—not muscle, sinew, or bone—and so long as the cuts do not hurt the quality of service. But sometimes they do affect service, of course, because now and then the only way for a company to know it's gone too far is to go there.

If service does begin to slip, beware the deadly temptation to "fix" the problem by sweeping it under the rug. Among the traits McKinsey and Company listed for firms headed for trouble is the tendency to "measure satisfaction in a way that intends to be flattering to the company."

Ask Your Customers, but Ask the Right Questions

Of course the only perception of service that really matters is what customers think, and virtually all telecommunications companies sample their customers. The objective of such surveys, however, should be to look for *problems* (which should be thought of as "opportunities to improve"), not for the "right" answers.

This was beautifully illustrated by a sign in a small deli: "We appreciate your compliments but it is more important for us to hear your criticisms." Make sure your company's service measurements are geared toward uncovering opportunities to improve rather than downplaying them.

Ask the People who Provide the Service

These largely unsung heroes and heroines are, without question, the stalwarts of any business. They represent your company day after day, greeting the customer with a smile and a "can do" attitude...or so you hope.

To create a satisfying experience for the customer these people must feel good about what they do and good about themselves for doing it. They must take pride in their jobs and in their contribution. They must feel that only through their truly helping and serving the customer will the company benefit.

Conversely, if they feel forced to cut corners on the quality of their service to customers they will probably not feel very good about what they do. When this happens, every single day becomes a long, hard struggle to push the same darn boulder up the same darn mountain. Take care of the people in the trenches and they will take care of you!

Conclusion: Make Service Your Mission

Excellent, first-rate service—there is no better preparation for the uncertain future than to legitimately rate an A+ in this critical area. Make it your mission and your passion, and the future will largely take care of itself.

Appendix: Your Personal Service History

The telephone business was made great by the collective efforts of the individual men and women who worked together to provide the best customer service in the world. This section of *In the Spirit of Service* uniquely combines your personal history of telephone service in the same book as that of Alexander Graham Bell and the other industry founders. If you are a telephone employee or veteran—or both—and will take a few minutes to complete this section you will have done a great thing not only for your descendants but for the history and heritage of the industry as well.

Think about it. If you had the opportunity to receive similar information on your parents or grandparents, or on *their* ancestors, you would probably cherish it as one of your most valuable heirlooms and possessions. Learning about the human side of our ancestors provides us a sense of stability, of heritage, of belonging. Just think what it will mean to your descendants to read this book years from now and really understand what the spirit of service was all about in the business you chose for your life's work. It will only take a few minutes to complete this section and thereby produce a gift and heirloom that may rank with the most important marks you make on this Earth.

Your name and Social Security Number:

_____

Your birthdate and birthplace:

_____

Your parents' names, birthdates, and birthplaces:

_____

_____

Where did you grow up?

_____

Names and birthdates of your children:

_____

_____

_____

_____

Names and birthdates of your grandchildren:

_____

_____

_____

_____

_____

_____

When and where did you start in the telecommunications business? How did you come to be hired?

_____

_____

_____

_____

What was your first job with the company?

_____

_____

_____

What sort of training did you have?

_____

_____

_____

Did you like the job? Why or why not?

_____

_____

_____

_____

_____

_____

What were some of your favorite jobs, and why?

_____

_____

_____

_____

_____

_____

_____

_____

_____

_____

_____

_____

_____

_____

_____

_____

_____

What do you remember about service or procedures in the early days that are much different now? Do you think things are better or worse now?

_____

_____

_____

_____

_____

_____

_____

_____

_____

_____

_____

_____

_____

_____

_____

_____

_____

_____

Were you ever involved with doing your job during or after a natural disaster? What were the circumstances?

_____

_____

_____

_____

_____

_____

_____

_____

_____

_____

_____

_____

_____

_____

_____

_____

_____

_____

Are you a member of the Telephone Pioneers of America, or another community service organization? Which one?

_____

_____

_____

If so, what are some of the community service activities and projects you enjoy most?

_____

_____

_____

_____

_____

_____

_____

_____

_____

_____

_____

_____

_____

_____

_____

Other information you wish to add.

_____

_____

_____

_____

_____

_____

_____

_____

_____

_____

_____

_____

_____

_____

_____

_____

_____

Acknowledgments

Much of the flavor and content of this book would not have been possible without the work of Dr. Robert V. Bruce for his 1973 biography, *Bell: Alexander Graham Bell and the Conquest of Solitude.* Dr. Bruce's book, available through Cornell University Press, is undisputed as the authoritative biography of the inventor. The influence of Dr. Bruce's research and skillful writing is evident throughout the sections of *In the Spirit of Service* concerning both Alexander Graham Bell and Gardiner Hubbard. Dr. Bruce won the 1988 Pulitzer Prize for History for *The Launching of Modern American Science, 1846-1876*, also available from Cornell University Press.

We are grateful to Jack Stephens, Aynsley MacFarlane, and the rest of the staff of the Alexander Graham Bell National Historic Site at Baddeck, Cape Breton Island, Nova Scotia. Their helpfulness in providing photographs and other information regarding the inventor was invaluable, and their hospitality was superb. Bell's majestic home at Beinn Bhreagh may be seen from the museum, across the beautiful Bras d'Or lake. The three buildings of the spacious, modern museum, under the direction of the Canadian Parks Service, house a treasure of Bell artifacts, papers, and other memorabilia, much of it related to his fascinating work in the productive years following the invention of the telephone. More information may be obtained by calling (902) 295-2069.

We owe a debt of gratitude to numerous officers and administrators of the Telephone Pioneers of America around the U.S. and Canada, and to the Pioneer Association, for providing suggestions and feedback, both positive and critical, as to the direction and contents of this book. We also very much appreciate the involvement of Mr. Irv Fries in this regard.

The staff of Henning Communications of St. Louis provided top-notch design, layout, and art direction. We are also grateful to friends and associates who helped with the creation of the title and for contributing other helpful suggestions, including Pat Golden, Dan Baker, Jim Kistner, Elizabeth Merz, Mike Herron, Corine Duft, and Pat Galicia.

Our wives and partners, Jan Velayas and Deanna Frailey, provided unconditional support, encouragement, and a sense of humor at all times. Ryan and Jon Frailey stuffed a lot of envelopes, and we appreciate their not turning us in for child labor law violations.

Finally, the authors would like to acknowledge each other's friendship in a great partnership that withstood the test of numerous discussions and negotiation. The end result is indeed a collaborative effort, and we hope you enjoyed reading it as much as we enjoyed its creation.

Photographic Credits

Alexander Graham Bell National Historic Site
AT&T Photo Archives
Bell Canada
Telephone Pioneers of America

Excerpt from *You Can't Afford the Luxury of a Negative Thought*, by John-Roger and Peter McWilliams, published by Prelude Press, 8159 Santa Monica Boulevard, Los Angeles, California, 90046, 1-800-LIFE-101.

Excerpts from *Telephone: The First Hundred Years*, by John Brooks, published by Harper-Collins, New York.

Excerpts from *In One Man's Life*, by Albert Bigelow Paine, published by Harper-Collins, New York.

Excerpts from *Exploring Life*, by Thomas Watson, published by D. Appleton and Company, New York.

Bibliography

Books

Boettinger, H.M. *The Telephone Book: Bell, Watson, Vail and American Life 1876-1976.* Croton-on-Hudson, New York, Riverwood Publishers Limited, 1977.

Brooks, John. *Telephone: The First Hundred Years.* New York, Harper & Row, 1976.

Bruce, Robert V. *Bell: Alexander Graham Bell and the Conquest of Solitude.* Ithaca, Cornell University Press, 1973.

Coll, Steve. *The Deal of the Century: The Breakup of AT&T.* New York, Altheneum, 1986.

Fetherstonhaugh, R.C. *Charles Fleetford Sise: 1834-1918.* Montreal, Gazette Printing Company, Ltd., 1944.

Hackenburg, Herbert J. *Muttering Machines to Laser Beams: A History of Mountain Bell.* Denver, Mountain Bell, 1986.

Kleinfield, Sonny. *The Biggest Company on Earth: A Profile of AT&T.* New York, Holt, Rinehart, and Winston, 1981.

Kraus, Constantine Raymond; and Duerig, Alfred W. *The Rape of Ma Bell: The Criminal Wrecking of the Best Telephone System in the World.* Secaucus, New Jersey, Lyle Stuart, Inc., 1988.

Paine, Albert Bigelow. *In One Man's Life: Being Chapters from the Personal & Business Career of Theodore N. Vail.* New York, Harper Brothers, 1921.

Park, David G., Jr. *Good Connections: A Century of Service by the Men and Women of Southwestern Bell*. St. Louis, Southwestern Bell, 1984.

Pool, Ithiel de Sola. *The Social Impact of the Telephone*. Cambridge, The MIT Press, 1977.

Temin, Peter; and Galambos, Louis. *The Fall of the Bell System*. Cambridge, Cambridge University Press, 1987.

Toward, Lilias M. *Mabel Bell: Alexander's Silent Partner*. Toronto, Methuen Publications, 1984.

Watson, Thomas A. *Exploring Life*. New York, D. Appleton and Company, 1926.

Yanekian, Adrienne. *The Telephone Pioneers of America: 1911-1961*. New York, The Telephone Pioneers of America, 1961.

Periodicals

Ameritech Corporation Annual Reports, 1984-1992.

AT&T Corporation Annual Reports, 1984-1992.

Bell Atlantic Corporation Annual Reports, 1984-1992.

BellSouth Corporation Annual Reports, 1984-1992.

Brandweek, Publisher's Note, March 15, 1993.

NYNEX Corporation Annual Reports, 1984-1992.

Pacific Telesis Corporation Annual Reports, 1984-1992.

Southwestern Bell Corporation Annual Reports, 1984-1992.

Telephony, March 15, 1992.

U S West Corporation Annual Reports, 1984-1992.

Index

intelligible sentence 29; first commercial line, 84; growth of business 34; patenting 35, 84, 120.

Telephone Pioneers of America, 147-177.

Telephonic probe, ILLUS. 54; invention of, 53-54; and Dr. Girdner, 55.

Twain, Mark, 65, 68.

U.S. census, 51-52.

U S West Corporation, 269-279.

Vacuum jacket, 60.

Vail, Alfred, 78, 79.

Vail, Theodore N., ILLUS. 76, 79, 92, 98, 105, 109; ancestry, 77-78; and Bell Telephone of Canada, 130, 132; and efficient mail delivery, 81-83; health, 98; is hired by Bell Company, 35, 86; innovations under, 107-110; in Iowa, 79-80; management philosophy, 89-90, 97-98, 103-107; moves office to Boston, 94; and New York Telephone, 87-88; passage, 114, personal tragedies, 102; resigns from telephone business, 100; returns to AT&T, 103; and serenity 89, 91; and South America, 101; and Speedwell Farms, 99-100,106; as telegraph operator, 79; and (Harry) Thayer, 113; Vail Medal created, 114; and Western Union management, 110-111; in Wyoming, 80-81.

Visible Speech, 45.

Volta Prize, 52.

Volta Review, 53.

Watson, Thomas A., ILLUS. 18, 37, 39, 109; as actor and playwright 39; birth 20; meets AGB, 23; builds first telephone, 28; contracts with AGB, 29; development of call bell, 97; education, 21, 36; and farming, 38; and Fore River company, 38; and geology, 38; loses telephone fortune, 38; and telephone patents, 29; meets Vail, 34; passage, 40; on perseverance, 30; reflections on AGB, 31, 33; on Sanders as treasurer, 32; after the telephone, 36-40; and transcontinental telephone call, 40.

Western Union, purchase of multiple telegraphy rights, 119; refuses to buy telephone patents 30, 84; violates patents 85, 88, 93; reaches agreement with Bell Company, 93-94; Vail as president, 110-111.

Williams, Charles (Williams's Machine Shop), 22, 25, 86.